CALVIN COOLIDGE
1872-1933

Chronology · Documents · Bibliographical Aids

Edited by
Philip R. Moran

Series Editor
Howard F. Bremer

1970
OCEANA PUBLICATIONS, INC.
Dobbs Ferry, New York

Library of Congress Catalog Card Number: 74-116060
International Standard Book Number: 0-379-12079-8

To Teri and Angela, charming collaborators
in delving into the past.

Manufactured in the United States of America

CONTENTS 105773

EDITOR'S FOREWORD

Every attempt has been made to cite the most accurate dates in this Chronology. Diaries, documents, and similar evidence have been used to determine the exact date. If, however, later scholarship has found such dates to be obviously erroneous, the more plausible date has been used. Should this Chronology be in conflict with other authorities, the student is urged to go back to original sources.

This is a research tool compiled primarily for the student. While it does make some judgments on the significance of the events, it is hoped that they are reasoned judgments based on a long acquaintance with American History.

Obviously, the very selection of events by any writer is itself a judgment.

The essence of these little books is in their making available some pertinent facts and key documents plus a critical bibliography which should direct the student to investigate for himself additional and/or contradictory material. The works cited may not always be available in small libraries, but neither are they usually the old, out of print type of books often included in similar accounts. Documents in this volume are taken from: the Congressional Record: United States Reports, Supreme Court, and State Department Papers Relating to the Foreign Relations of the United States.

CHRONOLOGY

EARLY LIFE AND CAREER

1872

July 4

Born, Plymouth, Vermont. Father: John Calvin Coolidge. Mother: Victoria Josephine Moor Coolidge. Forbears had lived in Plymouth since 1781. Named John Calvin, he dropped the John after graduating from college.

1875

April 15

Sister, Abigail Gratia, born.

1876

Father, prospering, bought new home (in which Coolidge later took oath of office as President).

1877

December

Started schooling at Plymouth Notch.

1880

Father, a farmer and storekeeper, served as town superintendent of schools. He later held many other public offices.

1885

March 14

Mother died.

1887

Autumn

Enrolled at Black River Academy, Ludlow, Vermont.

1890

March 6

Sister died, probably of appendicitis.

May 23

Graduated from academy in a class of five boys and four girls.

Autumn

Took entrance examinations for Amherst College.

A bad cold prevented him from completing the examinations.

1891

Spring

Studied two months at St. Johnsbury Academy in Vermont and received college entrance certificate.

September 9

Father remarried, to Caroline Athelia Brown, a Plymouth school teacher. Much affection developed between her and her stepson.

September 17

Entered Amherst.

1894

September 21

Elected Grove Orator by his classmates to give humorous speech at commencement activities.

1895

June 26

Graduated cum laude from Amherst in class of 76.

Autumn

Began to read law with firm of John C. Hammond and Henry P. Field in Northampton, Massachusetts. Took first small steps into politics by handing out ballots in Field's successful bid for post of mayor of Northampton.

1896

Attended Republican convention at Chester as alternate delegate.

1897

July 2

Admitted to Massachusetts bar.
Selected to serve on Republican city committee of Northampton.

1898

February 1

Opened own law office in Masonic Building.

October

Delegate to Republican convention at South Deerfield.

December 6	Elected city councilman from Ward 2.

1900
January 18	Elected city solicitor.

1901
January 17	Re-elected city solicitor.

1902
January 16	Defeated by Democrat Theobald M. Connor in third election bid to be city solicitor.

1903
June 4	Appointed temporary clerk of courts for Hampshire County. Did not seek election in autumn to full term in position, and served until January 1, 1904.

1904
Named as chairman of the Republican city committee.

1905
October 4	Married Grace Anna Goodhue at Burlington, Vermont, in her home. They had met in Northampton, where she taught at Clarke Institute for the Deaf.
December 5	Defeated in election for school committeeman.

1906
August	Rented half of two-family house at 21 Massasoit Street. He continued to rent it throughout his years in public office and returned there after leaving White House.
September 7	Son John born in Northampton.
November 6	Elected to Massachusetts house of representatives, the General Court. Took room in Boston and returned home on weekends. Became known as reliable follower of Massachusetts Republican leader Winthrop Murray Crane.

1907

November 5   Re-elected representative in close battle, and served second and final term.

1908

April 13   Calvin Coolidge, Jr., born.

1909

December 7   Elected mayor of Northampton. When term began the following January 3, he started an uninterrupted career in public office that would end when he left the White House.

1910

December 6   Re-elected mayor.

1911

November 7   Elected state senator. During term he was chairman of a legislative committee that helped bring settlement of Lawrence textile strike. He continued to work in Boston weekdays and return to Northampton on weekends.

1912

November 5   Re-elected state senator. Served as chairman of committee on railroads.

1913

November 4   Re-elected to a third term as senator and elected senate president in January. On taking position, he gave his "Have Faith in Massachusetts" speech, considered best example of his philosophy.

1914

November 3   Re-elected state senator. In January, again elected senate president. His 42-word address stressed, "Be brief."

1915

November 2   Elected lieutenant-governor by 52,000 votes over Edward P. Barry, Democrat.

1916

January 6   Inaugurated as lieutenant-governor. Samuel W. McCall became governor.

November 7   Re-elected lieutenant-governor.

1917

November 6   Again elected lieutenant-governor.

1918

November 5   Elected governor of Massachusetts by a majority of 16,000. He was inaugurated the following January 2. Channing H. Cox was lieutenant-governor.

1919

February 24   Welcomed President Woodrow Wilson to Boston on the latter's return from the Paris Peace Conference.

May 20   Lawrence, Massachusetts, textile strike resolved, partly through Coolidge's efforts.

July 29   Edwin U. Curtis, Boston's police commissioner, issued a general order forbidding police to unionize.

August 11   Boston Police Union chartered. Subsequently, Curtis charged 19 leaders with insubordination. Under threat of a police strike if union officers were penalized, the 19 were found guilty but sentences were postponed.

September 3   Coolidge declined to intervene in the dispute.

September 8   Curtis suspended the 19. The police voted, 1134 to 2, to strike the next day.

September 9	In late afternoon, 1117 policemen struck. Disorder and looting followed in Boston. Prior to walkout, Coolidge had again declined to intervene on Curtis' assurance that there was no need for emergency measures.
September 10	Mayor Andrew J. Peters, who had been trying to find a solution to the dispute, now took command, called out state guardsmen in the Boston area, and asked the governor for three more regiments.
September 11	The disorders largely over, Coolidge took charge and ordered out the entire state guard. Curtis dismissed all 1117 strikers, none of whom were rehired.
September 14	In telegram answering Samuel Gompers, president of the American Federation of Labor, Coolidge made statement which helped bring him national acclaim: "There is no right to strike against the public safety by anybody, anywhere, any time."
September 23	Renominated for governorship in party primary.
September 24	Issued a strong statement on public security in which he opposed rehiring of strikers.
October 4	Nominated for re-election at Republican state convention.
October 10	"Have Faith in Massachusetts," Coolidge speeches, published.
November 4	Re-elected governor by a big majority. That fall there were first references to him as a potential presidential candidate, including a November 14 Literary Digest article.

1920

January 16	Prohibition went into effect.

May 18   Stepmother died in Plymouth, Vermont.

June 8   Republican national convention opened in Chicago
                with Senator Henry Cabot Lodge as chairman.

June 11   Nominated for presidency, among lesser of 18 nom-
                inees.

June 12   Harding nominated for presidency, after deadlock
                among major candidates General Leonard Wood,
                Frank O. Lowden and Hiram Johnson. Coolidge nom-
                inated by Wallace McCamant of Oregon for vice-
                president. Selected over Irvine L. Lenroot of Wis-
                consin, 674 1/2 to 146 1/2, in a surge of enthusiasm
                by delegates eager to return home from hot and costly
                Chicago.

July 27   Officially notified of nomination in ceremony at Smith
                College in Northampton.

November 2   Harding and Coolidge elected by a landslide vote over
                Democrats James M. Cox, for president, and Frank-
                lin Delano Roosevelt, running against Coolidge.

December 17   Coolidges visited Harding in Marion, Ohio.

                                1921

January 6   Term as governor ended. Channing H. Cox, elected
                the previous November, succeeded him.

                        VICE PRESIDENCY

March 4   Took oath as Vice President in the Senate Chamber.
                Delivered very short inaugural speech to the Senate
                on "the great value of a deliberative body as a safe-
                guard of our liberties," as he wrote later in his Au-
                tobiography. He attended the inauguration of Presi-
                dent Warren G. Harding on the east portico of the
                Capitol.

March 8   Attended first meeting of Harding's Cabinet.

April 28   Gave speech at Carnegie Institute in Pittsburgh.

May 28   Elected life trustee of Amherst.

May 31   Harding issued executive order transferring Naval
                 oil lands to the Secretary of the Interior. Teapot
                 Dome scandal developed from this beginning.

November 12   Washington Disarmament Conference opened.

1922

April 7   Secretary of the Interior Albert B. Fall secretly
                 leased the Teapot Dome oil reserve to oilman Henry
                 F. Sinclair.

April 15   When Teapot Dome leasing became known, Senator
                 John B. Kendrick of Wyoming introduced a resolution
                 seeking an explanation of the action.

April 29   Senate adopted a resolution introduced by Robert La-
                 Follette calling for investigation of the oil leases.

September 19   Harding vetoed a veterans bonus bill, as Coolidge
                 was also to do later as President.

September 23   Attended Massachusetts Republican convention in
                 Boston.

November 22   Scandal in Veterans Bureau began to surface. Fol-
                 lowing allegations of graft, Harding ordered halt to
                 sales of surplus goods at Bureau warehouse in Per-
                 ryville, Maryland, on this date.

1923

January 2	Harding accepted resignation of Secretary of the Interior Fall, effective March 4.
February 1	Charles F. Cramer, Veterans Bureau counsel, resigned. Bureau reorganization announced.
February 12	Senate ordered investigation of Veterans Bureau.
February 15	Charles R. Forbes resigned as director of Veterans Bureau. He was later to be convicted of accepting graft.
February 24	Harding asked Senate consent for the United States to join World Court, with reservations proposed by Secretary of State Charles E. Hughes. Coolidge as President supported Harding's proposal, against opposition of the Senate.
March 4	Coolidges left Washington at conclusion of session of 67th Congress. Traveled to Virginia and Massachusetts.
March 14	As Senate investigation of Veterans Bureau neared, Cramer committed suicide.
April 9	Supreme Court, in Adkins v. Children's Hospital, ruled that the Minimum Wage Act of 1918 in District of Columbia violated due process.
April 25	Coolidges attended funeral of her father, Andrew L. Goodhue, in Burlington, Vermont.
May 30	Jess W. Smith, rumored as involved in graft in connection with his White House activities, committed suicide.
June 20	Harding set out on extensive trip to the West Coast, Canada and Alaska.

| June | As Amherst trustee, Coolidge participated in request for resignation of Alexander Meiklejohn, who had introduced highly liberal views to the college as its president. |

July 8   Coolidges returned to Plymouth.

August 2 Harding died in San Francisco.

PRESIDENCY

August 3 Took oath of office at 2:47 a.m. by the light of an oil lamp in the sitting room of the Coolidge farm in Plymouth. Oath administered by his father, Colonel John Calvin Coolidge, a notary public. In morning Coolidge left for Washington.

August 7 Harding funeral train, with his body, arrived in Washington.

August 10 Attended Harding funeral in Marion, Ohio. Returning to Washington, Coolidge continued to stay at New Willard until August 21. He then moved into the White House.

August 13 George Harvey resigned as Ambassador to Great Britain.

August 14 Held first regular Cabinet meeting. He retained Harding appointees: Charles E. Hughes of New York, State; Andrew W. Mellon of Pennsylvania, Treasury; Henry C. Wallace of Iowa, Agriculture; Herbert C. Hoover of California, Commerce; Harry S. New of Indiana, Postmaster General; John W. Weeks of Massachusetts, War; Harry M. Daugherty of Ohio, Attorney General; Hubert Work of Colorado, Interior; Edwin Denby of

Michigan, Navy; and James J. Davis of Pennsylvania, Labor. Mellon, Davis and New remained in posts until Coolidge left office, and Hoover until his nomination for Presidency in 1928.

August 15   Brought coal miners and owners together in unsuccessful attempt to avoid a threatened strike.

August 21   Proclaimed the five-power naval treaty that had been signed February 6, 1922.
Took oath of office a second time, administered by Justice Adolph A. Hoehling of the Supreme Court of the District of Columbia, at the New Willard. Attorney General Daugherty had doubted validity of oath administered by Coolidge's father.

August 24   Named Governor Gifford Pinchot of Pennsylvania as special mediator in the coal strike.

September 1   Coal strike began.

September 7   Agreement reached in coal strike. The mines reopened on September 19.

September 10   Signed convention with Mexico regarding claims arising from revolutionary acts from 1910 to 1920. The convention was proclaimed on February 23, 1924.

October 22   Senate investigation of Veterans Bureau scandal opened. This led to trial and conviction of Forbes and businessman John W. Thompson for conspiracy to defraud the government.

October 23   Senate Committee on Public Lands and Surveys opened hearings on the oil leases. Former Secretary Fall was first to testify. Senator Thomas J. Walsh of Montana was main questioner at hearings.

October 25   Secretary Denby questioned by senators at Teapot

Dome inquiry. Sinclair was called four days later.

December 3   Edward L. Doheny questioned on Elk Hills (California) oil lease Fall had given him.

December 6   Sixty-eighth Congress session opened. Touched on wide range of topics in first annual message to Congress.

December 8   Admitted at Gridiron Club dinner in Washington that he was seeking nomination in 1924. Various indications at this time showed he led field for the nomination.

December 10   Spoke over radio for the first time from the White House.

December 15   Names Charles G. Dawes, Henry M. Robinson and Owen D. Young to a commission to study Germany's default of reparations payments.

December 26   Fall wrote Senate investigating committee that $100,-000 he had received was not a bribe from Doheny or Sinclair, but had come as a loan from publisher Edward B. McLean.

1924

January 17   Addressed American Society of Newspaper Editors.

January 24   Doheny on stand admitted that the $100,000 in cash received by Fall was from him, as a "loan."

January 28   In Senate, Walsh called for resignation of Secretary of Navy Denby.

January 29   Senator Burton K. Wheeler introduced resolution asking Coolidge to seek Daugherty's resignation.

February 2   Fall refused to testify before Senate committee.

February 3   Woodrow Wilson died after illness and paralysis dat-
                  ing from September, 1919, collapse.

February 8   Joint Congressional resolution ordered that oil leases
                  be annulled and canceled.

February 11   In 47-34 vote, Senate tried to force Coolidge to oust
                  Denby. Coolidge saw this as an infringement of Presi-
                  dential rights.

February 12   In New York City speech before the National Repub-
                  lican Club, Coolidge supported the Mellon Plan for
                  income tax reduction and asserted that he intended
                  to insure that American lives and rights would be pro-
                  tected in accordance with international law.

February 18   Denby's resignation, effective March 10, was an-
                  nounced.

March 12   Senate committee investigating Daugherty began hear-
                  ings.

March 18   Appointed Curtis S. Wilbur of California as Secretary
                  of Navy.

March 21   Ratified convention with Great Britain on prevention
                  of smuggling of intoxicating liquor. One of a number
                  of such treaties negotiated in this period. The agree-
                  ment permitted search and possible seizure outside
                  the three-mile limit, up to an hour's traveling distance
                  of the suspected vessel. Proclaimed May 22.

March 24   Sinclair cited by Senate for contempt in refusing to
                  answer questions.

March 28   Demanded and received Daugherty's resignation, os-
                  tensibly for refusal to give certain files to the Senate
                  investigators.

April 2   Appointed Harlan F. Stone to succeed Daugherty as Attorney General.

April 9   Dawes Plan on payment of debts by Germany announced.

April 10   William M. Butler said Coolidge was certain of nomination on the first ballot.

April 22   Outlined platform proposals in speech at Associated Press luncheon in New York City.

April 23   Senate passed bonus bill.

April 28   Dedicated National Academy of Sciences building in Washington.

May 10-13   Socialist Labor Party meeting in New York City nominated Frank T. Johns of Oregon for President and Verne L. Reynolds of New York for Vice President.

May 13   Vetoed Bursum Pension Bill.

May 15   Vetoed bonus bill.

May 17   House passed bonus bill over Coolidge's veto by 313-78 vote.

May 19   Senate overrode bonus bill veto, 59-26.

May 24   Gave address at Confederate Memorial in Arlington National Cemetery.

May 26   Signed Immigration Act of 1924 which excluded Orientals. This act gave great offense to the Japanese particularly.

May 27	Signed Rogers Act reorganizing diplomatic and consular service.
May	Named William M. Butler as chairman of the National Republican Committee.
May	Teapot Dome hearings adjourned.
June 2	Signed Simmons-Longworth tax bill. Signed bill granting Indians full citizenship.
June 3	McNary-Haugen bill has first defeat, in House.
June 3-4	American Party meeting in Columbus, Ohio, nominated Gilbert O. Nations of Washington, D.C., for President, and Charles H. Randall of California for Vice President.
June 4-6	Prohibition Party meeting in Columbus, Ohio, nominated Herman P. Faris of Missouri for President and Marie C. Brehm of California for Vice President.
June 7	First session of 68th Congress ended.
June 10	Republican national convention opened at Cleveland, Ohio. Senator Frank W. Mondell named chairman.
June 12	Nominated on first ballot with 1065 out of total 1109 votes. General Charles G. Dawes of Illinois nominated for Vice President. Secretary of State Kellogg warned Mexico on matter of American safety and property rights with regard to oil expropriations. Angered Mexican authorities imposed further restrictions as a result.
June 17-19	The Farmer Labor Party nominated Duncan McDonald for President and William Bouck for Vice President. Convention was in St. Paul, Minnesota.

June 24-July 9   Democrats balloted 103 times before nominating John Davis of West Virginia for President and Charles W. Bryan of Nebraska for Vice President at convention in New York City, the longest such convention of a major political party.

June 30   Washington, D.C., grand jury indicted Fall, Sinclair, Doheny and Doheny's son on charges of conspiracy to defraud the government and charged Fall with bribery.

July 1   Rogers Bill went into effect.

July 4   Senator Robert M. LaFollette of Wisconsin nominated for President by Progressive Party meeting at Cleveland, with Senator Burton K. Wheeler of Montana for a running mate.

July 6-8   Socialist Party meeting in Cleveland supported La-Follette and Wheeler.

July 7   Calvin Coolidge, Jr., died in Washington from blood poisoning of the foot.

July 10   Attended service in Northampton for his son.

July 11   Workers Party nominated William Z. Foster of New York for President and Benjamin Gitlow of New York for Vice President at St. Paul, Minnesota, convention.

August 14   Notified of nomination at formal ceremony in Memorial Continental Hall in Washington.

August 16   Germany and Allies sign "Dawes Plan."

September 6   Gave speech on aid to Europe at dedication of statue of Lafayette in Baltimore. Coolidge's campaign theme was "Keep Cool with Coolidge."

October 4   Helped dedicate monument to First Division of World
                   War I expeditionary force.

October 25   Henry C. Wallace, Secretary of Agriculture, died.

November 4   Coolidge elected by largest Republican plurality in
                   history, with 15,725,016 votes to Davis' 8,386,503
                   and LaFollette's 4,822,856. He received 382 elec-
                   toral votes (35 states) to Davis' 136 (12 states) and
                   LaFollette's 13 (1 state).

November 9   Henry Cabot Lodge died.

November 21   Mrs. Harding died.

                   Howard M. Gore of West Virginia appointed Secre-
                   tary of Agriculture.

December 2   Senator Oscar Underwood of Alabama, with Coolidge's
                   support, proposed bill to lease Muscle Shoals to pri-
                   vate industry.

December 3   Sent annual message to Congress.

December 4   Addressed the Chicago Commercial Club.

                              1925

January 5   Secretary of State Hughes submitted resignation.

January 10   Nominated Charles B. Warren of Michigan as Attor-
                   ney General.

January 14   Underwood bill to lease Muscle Shoals adopted by
                   Senate after similar action in the House of Represent-
                   atives. However, Senator George Norris, who favored
                   government operation of the facility, blocked enact-
                   ment.

January 15   C. Bascom Slemp retired as Coolidge's secretary.

January 25   James R. Sheffield confirmed as ambassador to Mexico.

February 4   Colonel Charles K. Forbes, former director of Veteran's Bureau, convicted of defrauding the government. He was sentenced to two years in the penitentiary and a $10,000 fine.

February 5   Senate confirmed appointment of Harlan F. Stone to Supreme Court following resignation of Associate Justice Joseph McKenna.

February 16   Frank B. Kellogg approved to succeed Hughes as Secretary of State on March 4.

February 18   Appointed William M. Jardine of Kansas as Secretary of Agriculture, to take office March 4.

March 3   House approved plan to join World Court by a vote of 303-28.

SECOND TERM

March 4   Coolidge inaugurated. His second term Cabinet consisted of Mellon, Weeks, New, Wilbur, Work, Hoover, Davis, Kellogg and Jardine. Coolidge's oath was administered by Chief Justice William Howard Taft. Inaugural speech was the first to be broadcast. Vice President Dawes at his induction in Senate strongly criticized filibuster practice.
                    A special session of the Senate opened, to last until March 18.
                    Everett Sanders became Coolidge's secretary.

March 10   Senate rejected appointment of Warren, 41-39. Dawes, napping at his hotel, arrived in Senate chamber too late to break a 40-40 tie, a situation changed meanwhile by a switch of one vote.

March 16   Senate again rejected Warren, 46-39.

March 17   John Garibaldi Sargent of Vermont unanimously con-
                firmed by Senate as Attorney General.

March 23   Ratified treaty with Cuba giving that country title to
                Isle of Pines. Treaty proclaimed March 24, 1925.

April 7   Ratified convention between the U.S. and Central
                American republics establishing international com-
                mission of inquiry. Proclaimed June 15, 1925.

May 28   In Los Angeles, judge ruled that Elk Hills oil lease
                was null and void because Doheny fraudulently gave
                Fall $100,000.

June 1   Ratified convention with Dominican Republic concern-
                ing prior withdrawal of Marines. Convention signed
                June 30, 1922, and proclaimed December 8, 1925.

June 18   Senator LaFollette died.

June 19   Judge T. Blake Kennedy in Cheyenne, Wyoming, called
                Teapot Dome lease valid, but was later overruled.

June 22   Coolidges vacationed at Summer White House in
                Swampscott, Massachusetts.

July 2   Kellogg called for indemnity settlements from Mex-
                ico for seized property of Americans.

July 3   In Massachusetts speech, Coolidge supported Locar-
                no agreements.

July 10-21   At trial in Dayton, Tennessee, John T. Scopes tried
                and convicted of violating state law prohibiting teach-
                ing of evolution. Clarence Darrow defended him.
                William Jennings Bryan, prosecutor, died on July 26.

August 5   Proclaimed nine-power treaty concerning China, signed February 6, 1922.

September 12   Appointed Dwight Morrow to aircraft inquiry board, to determine best use of aircraft for defense and examine Colonel "Billy" Mitchell's charges of unpreparedness.

October 13   Dwight F. Davis of Missouri appointed Secretary of War to succeed Weeks.

October 28   Gave address at dedication of monument in Washington to General Jose de San Martin, given by Argentina.

October 28-   Colonel William "Billy" Mitchell tried for his accusations that air power was being "almost treasonably" neglected. Found guilty, he was suspended for five years but resigned instead. In 1942 he was posthumously honored by government for his warnings.
December 17

November 14   Part of Italy's war debt canceled and interest rate reduced.

November 19   Gave speech to New York State Chamber of Commerce in New York City in which he praised business as a great contribution to "moral and spiritual advancement of the race."

December 7   In speech to American Farm Bureau Federation in Chicago, Coolidge said government should not fix farm prices.
                    First session of 69th Congress opened.

December 8   Presented third annual message to Congress.

December 9   In budget message to Congress, Coolidge asked for appropriation for aviation.

1926

January 16   New McNary-Haugen Bill introduced in Senate. Named for Senator Charles L. McNary of Oregon and Congressman Gilbert H. Haugen of Iowa, bill sought federal board to control farm surpluses to keep prices steady.

January 27   Senate, 76-17, approved United States participation in World Court, with certain reservations. However, the United States never did join the court.

February 26   Signed Revenue Act reducing taxes.

March 17   Senate rejected Wallace McCamant of Oregon as federal judge. He had nominated Coolidge for Vice President in 1920.

March 18   Coolidge's father died.

March 21   Colonel Forbes began term in Leavenworth Penitentiary on Veterans Bureau conspiracy conviction.

April 6   Tacna-Arica Conference between Chile and Peru opened in Washington. As President, Coolidge was mediator in the dispute over ownership of two provinces. Coolidge called for a plebiscite, but the problem was not settled until 1929.

April 19   Addressed DAR in Washington.

April 29   United States and France signed debt repayment pact.

May 9   Richard E. Byrd and Floyd Bennett made first flight over the North Pole.

May 10   U.S. Marines land in Nicaragua in support of Adolfo Diaz as president. Marines left June 5.

May 18	Preparatory Commission for Geneva Disarmament Conference opened. Hugh S. Gibson was U.S. representative.
May 20	Signed Watson-Parker Bill creating a board of mediation in railway labor disputes.
May 25	Signed Public Buildings Act and Reclamation Relief Act.
July 2	Signed bill creating Army Air Corps. Distinguished Flying Cross established.
July 3	Congressional session ended. McNary-Haugen Bill stalemated.
July 5	Gave speech at celebration of the 150th anniversary of the Declaration of Independence in Philadelphia, in which he cautioned against radical changes in government. He then left for vacation in New York Adirondacks.
September 19	Returned to Washington.
September 22	Interview of Coolidge by Bruce Barton printed in New York Sun.
September 28	Cheyenne decision calling Teapot Dome lease valid was reversed.
October 21	Queen of Rumania visited the White House.
October 25	Myers v. U.S., Supreme Court ruled that a postmaster could be removed by the President without the consent of the Senate.
October 27	Addressed the American Association of Advertising Agencies in Washington, D.C.

November 17   Diaz Government in Nicaragua recognized by United States.

November 22   Fall and Doheny went on trial in District of Columbia Supreme Court. They were acquitted on December 16.

December 6   Second session of 69th Congress opened.

December 7   Sent fourth annual message to Congress.

1927

January 10   Explained intervention in Nicaragua in message to two houses of Congress.

January 12   Proclaimed Pan American treaty, signed May 3, 1923, at Santiago, Chile, designed to help avoid hemisphere conflicts.

January 17   Will Rogers visited White House.

January 25   Cyrus E. Woods appointed to Interstate Commerce Commission by Coolidge, but was rejected by Senate.

January 27   Senate recommended arbitration of dispute with Mexico over oil expropriations.
Kellogg issued "Statement of Policy" to Great Britain, which had urged joint action to protect nationals during Chinese incidents.

February 10   Called for naval armament conference, which met the following June 20.

February 22   Addressed joint session of Congress on 200th anniversary of birth of George Washington.

February 23   Signed Federal Radio Act.

February 25   Vetoed McNary-Haugen bill for first time.

February 28   Supreme Court upheld voiding of Doheny's Elk Hills oil lease.

March 3   Prohibition Bureau became part of Treasury Department.

March 4   Second session of 69th Congress ended on a filibuster. Daugherty acquitted of conspiracy to accept graft.

March 7   Sinclair trial on charge of contempt of Senate started in District of Columbia Supreme Court.
                     U.S. Supreme Court ruled unconstitutional a Texas law forbidding Negroes to vote in primaries.

March   Henry L. Stimson named envoy to Nicaragua after violence followed withdrawal of U.S. legation guard.

March 22   James T. Shotwell, Columbia University professor, proposed a French-American pact to outlaw war during visit with French Foreign Minister Aristide Briand.

April 6   Briand proposed publicly that pact be adopted. This came to be known as the Kellogg-Briand pact.

April 25   In New York City speech to United Press association, Coolidge outlines his policy regarding Mexico; said he believed nations had obligations to safeguard foreign visitors.

May 4   Stimson negotiated peace between opposing armies of Nicaragua's President Diaz and his rival, General Moncada.

May 20   Sinclair found guilty of contempt of Senate. Sentence was three months and $500 fine.

May 20-21	Charles A. Lindbergh flew non-stop to Paris.
June 11	Kellogg acknowledged Briand proposal. Lindbergh received Distinguished Flying Cross, the first recipient, during Washington visit.
June 13	Addressed First International Congress of Soil Science in Washington.
June 20	Briand draft of French-American pact to outlaw war submitted.
June-August	Coolidges vacationed in Black Hills of South Dakota.
June 20	Geneva naval disarmament conference opened. France and Italy sent no representatives, and Great Britain and the United States reached a stalemate on cruiser restrictions. Japan was represented. Adjourned August 4.
July 14	Named Dwight Morrow, Amherst classmate, to be ambassador to Mexico.
August 2	Issued statement, "I do not choose to run for President in nineteen twenty-eight," at Rapid City, South Dakota.
August 3	General Leonard Wood, Governor General of the Philippines, died. His successor was Henry L. Stimson.
August 17	Adopted by Sioux Indians. Gave speech to 10,000.
August 23	Nicola Sacco and Bartolomeo Vanzetti executed in Massachusetts on murder charges, after 1921 trial greatly criticized as biased.
August 31	Coolidges traveled to Yellowstone National Park, returning to Washington on September 11.

October 11   Supreme Court unanimously ruled the Teapot Dome lease invalid because fraudulently obtained.

October 13   Proclaimed convention extending General Claims Commission for Mexico.

October 17   Doheny-Fall conspiracy trial started.

October 19   Gave address at acceptance of monument of General George G. Meade at Washington.

October 23   Morrow arrived as ambassador in Mexico City. He was instrumental in re-establishing cordial relations between the two countries.

November 1   Doheny-Fall trial ended in mistrial because Doheny had jurors shadowed by Burns Agency detectives.

November 17   On suggestion of Morrow, Supreme Court of Mexico declared unconstitutional two articles of Petroleum Law, leading to resolution of disputes between Mexico and U.S. oil companies.

November 25   Signed International Radiotelegraph Convention. Pact was ratified by Coolidge on October 8, 1928, and proclaimed January 1, 1929.

December 5   Trial of Sinclair and Burns men for criminal contempt in jury shadowing started.
The 70th Congress opened first session.

December 6   Coolidge's annual message stressed tax and national debt reduction.

December 14   Colonel Lindbergh landed in Mexico City amid great enthusiasm after flight suggested by Morrow to help establish better U.S.-Mexican relations.

December 28   Mexican Congress enacted bill on oil concession rights that cleared way for agreement on the longstanding oil dispute.

Kellogg suggested that war outlawry pact be extended to all nations.

1928

January 6   Issued statement to newspapers saying he was not alarmed at increase of brokers' loans.

January 16   Gave opening address at Sixth International Conference of American States in Havana. U.S. blocked proposal criticizing interference by states in internal matters of other states, a reflection of U.S. intervention in Nicaragua.

January 24   Senate hearings on Teapot Dome scandal resumed.

February 4   Gave speech at dedication of new National Press Club in Washington.

February 21   Sinclair and three others convicted in jury shadowing.

March 1   Stimson arrived in Manila as Governor General.

March 13   Norris bill for government operation of Muscle Shoals passed by Senate.

April 5-21   Sinclair trial for conspiracy to defraud government ends in acquittal.

April 7   Ratified revision in International Sanitary Convention of January 17, 1912. Proclaimed June 21, 1928.

April 12   Senate again passed McNary-Haugen bill, 53-23.

May 2   Teapot Dome hearings concluded.

May 3   House passed McNary-Haugen bill.

May 5   Arbitration treaty with Germany signed. Ratified
                       May 15 by Coolidge.

May 15   Flood control bill signed by Coolidge.

May 22   Jones-White Act subsidizing American shipping and
                       mail contracts passed by Congress.

May 29   First session of 70th Congress ended. Signed revenue
                       act reducing income tax. Pocket veto of Coolidge
                       killed bill for government operation of Muscle Shoals.
                       Vetoed McNary-Haugen bill for second time.

June 12-15   Hoover nominated on first ballot at Republican na-
                       tional convention at Kansas City. Senator Charles
                       Curtis of Kansas named to run for Vice President.

June 26-29   Democrats meeting at Houston nominated New York
                       Governor Alfred E. Smith for President and Senator
                       Joseph T. Robinson of Arkansas for Vice President.

July 25   Roy O. West of Illinois became Secretary of the In-
                       terior, succeeding Hubert Work.

July   United States signed tariff treaty agreement with Na-
                       tionalist government of China, thus recognizing it.

August 16   Arbitration treaty with Austria signed. Coolidge rat-
                       ified it January 4, 1929, and proclaimed it February
                       28, 1929.

August 21   William F. Whiting of Massachusetts succeeded Hoo-
                       ver, who had resigned to campaign, as Secretary of
                       Commerce.

August 27   Kellogg-Briand Pact signed in Paris by 15 nations.
                       Ultimately 62 nations signed the treaty designed to
                       outlaw war as a way of settling international disputes.

September 12   Coolidge returned to Washington.

September 21   Gave brief speech at Bennington, Vermont, express-
                  ing his love for his native state.

October 19   Spoke at dedication of Fredericksburg and Spotsylva-
                  nia County battlefields memorial.

November 6   Hoover beat Smith, carrying 40 of 48 states.

December 3   Second session of 70th Congress opened.

December 4   Last annual message expressed great confidence in
                  continued prosperity of the country.

December 10   Addressed Pan American Conference of Arbitration
                  and Conciliation at Washington. Twenty nations at-
                  tended to seek ways to avoid disputes among them.

December 12   Addressed International Civil Aeronautics Confer-
                  ence in Washington.

December   Congress passed Boulder Dam Project Act.

                              1929

January 15   Kellogg-Briand Pact ratified by Senate 85-1.

January 17   Signed pact.

February 2   Federal Reserve Board warned on use of speculative
                  credit, in effort to control wild trading in stocks.

February 11   Committee on German reparations met in Paris and
                  devised Young reparations plan.

RETIREMENT

March 4	Hoover inaugurated. Coolidges returned to North-ampton. He joined Northampton Literary Club, was elected director of the New York Life Insurance Company in the spring, and saw his Autobiography published in serial form in Cosmopolitan magazine.
April 8	Supreme Court affirmed conviction of Sinclair for contempt of Congress. He began serving three-month term in Washington jail on May 6. In June his conviction for jury-shadowing was also upheld, adding to his time in jail, which ended on November 21.
June 21	Church-state agreement reached in Mexico through Morrow's efforts.
July 24	Attended luncheon with President Hoover at White House to celebrate signing of Kellogg-Briand Pact.
October 7	Trial of Fall began. He was convicted on October 25 of accepting a bribe. On November 1 he was sentenced to one year imprisonment plus $100,000 fine.
October 24	Stock market crashed.

1930

March 12-22	Doheny tried for bribing Fall and found not guilty by jury.
May 17	Coolidges moved into new home, "The Beeches." In previous month he had become president of American Antiquarian Society.
July 1	First daily article appeared in series Coolidge wrote for McClure Newspaper Syndicate.

1931

June 16

Attended dedication of memorial to Harding at Marion, Ohio.

July 20

Fall began serving sentence in New Mexico State Penitentiary. He was released May 9, 1932, and died in 1944.

October 5

Dwight Morrow died and Coolidge attended funeral.

October 6

Gave radio talk warning of certain kinds of insurance agents which led to a suit against him by a St. Louis agent. The suit was settled out of court.

1933

January 5

Died at Northampton of coronary thrombosis.

January 7

Funeral services at Edwards Congregational Church in Northampton brought thousands of mourners to the city. Buried at Plymouth Notch. Mrs. Coolidge lived until July 8, 1957.

DOCUMENTS

DOCUMENTS

FIRST ANNUAL MESSAGE
December 6, 1923

*Coolidge touched on a great variety of governmental af-
fairs, citing domestic problems as the main concern. He
pledged to enforce prohibition and stated his opposition
to reduction of war debts and to granting of a veterans'
bonus.*

Since the close of the last Congress the Nation has lost President Harding. The world knew his kindness and his humanity, his greatness and his character. He has left his mark upon history. He has made justice more certain and peace more secure. The surpassing tribute paid to his memory as he was borne across the continent to rest at last at home revealed the place he held in the hearts of the American people. But this is not the occasion for extended reference to the man or his work. In this presence, among those who knew and loved him, that is unnecessary. But we who were associated with him could not resume together the functions of our office without pausing for a moment, and in his memory reconsecrating ourselves to the service of our country. He is gone. We remain. It is our duty, under the inspiration of his example, to take up the burdens which he was permitted to lay down, and to develop and support the wise principles of government which he represented.

FOREIGN AFFAIRS

For us peace reigns everywhere. We desire to perpetuate it always by granting full justice to others and requiring of others full justice to ourselves.

Our country has one cardinal principle to maintain in its foreign policy. It is an American principle. It must be an American policy. We attend to our own affairs, conserve our own strength, and protect the interests of our own citizens; but we recognize thoroughly our obligation to help others, reserving to the decision of our own judgment the time, the place, and the method. We realize the common bond of humanity. We know the inescapable law of service.

Our country has definitely refused to adopt and ratify the covenant of the League of Nations. We have not felt warranted in assuming the responsibilities which its members have assumed. I am not proposing any change in this policy; neither is the Senate. The incident, so far as we are concerned, is closed. The League exists as a foreign agency. We hope it will be helpful. But the United States sees no reason to limit its own freedom and independence of action by joining it. We shall do well to recognize this basic fact in all national affairs and govern ourselves accordingly.

WORLD COURT

Our foreign policy has always been guided by two principles. The one is the avoidance of permanent political alliances which would sacrifice our proper independence. The other is the peaceful settlement of controversies between nations. By example and by treaty we have advocated arbitration. For nearly 25 years we have been a member of The Hague Tribunal, and have long sought the creation of a permanent World Court of Justice. I am in full accord with both of these policies. I favor the establishment of such a court intended to include the whole world. That is, and has long been, an American policy.

Pending before the Senate is a proposal that this Government give its support to the Permanent Court of International Justice, which is a new and somewhat different plan. This is not a partisan question. It should not assume an artificial importance. The court is merely a convenient instrument of adjustment to which we could go, but to which we could not be brought. It should be discussed with entire candor, not by a political but by a judicial method, without pressure and without prejudice. Partisanship has no place in our foreign relations. As I wish to see a court established, and as the proposal presents the only practical plan on which many nations have ever agreed, though it may not meet every desire, I therefore commend it to the favorable consideration of the Senate, with the proposed reservations clearly indicating our refusal to adhere to the League of Nations.

RUSSIA

Our diplomatic relations, lately so largely interrupted, are now being resumed, but Russia presents notable difficulties. We have every desire to see that great people, who are our traditional friends, restored to their position among the nations of the earth. We have relieved their pitiable destitution with an enormous charity. Our Government offers no objection to the carrying on of commerce by our citizens with the people of Russia. Our Government does not propose, however, to enter into relations with another regime which refuses to recognize the sancitity of international obligations. I do not propose to barter away for the privilege of trade any of the cherished rights of humanity. I do not propose to make merchandise of any American principles. These rights and principles must go wherever the sanctions of our Government go.

But while the favor of America is not for sale, I am willing to make very large concessions for the purpose of rescuing the people of Russia. Already encouraging evidences of returning to the ancient ways of society can be detected. But more are needed. Whenever there appears any disposition to compensate our citizens who were despoiled, and to recognize that debt contracted with our Government, not by the Czar, but by the newly formed Republic of Russia; whenever the active spirit of enmity to our institutions is abated; whenever there appear works mete for repentance; our country ought to be the first to go to the economic and moral rescue of Russia. We have every desire to help and no desire to injure. We hope the time is near at hand when we can act.

DEBTS

The current debt and interest due from foreign Governments, exclusive of the British debt of $4,600,000,000, is about $7,2000,000,-000. I do not favor the cancellation of this debt, but I see no objection to adjusting it in accordance with the principle adopted for the British debt. Our country would not wish to assume the role of an oppressive creditor, but would maintain the principle that financial obligations between nations are likewise moral obligations which international faith and honor require should be discharged.

Our Government has a liquidated claim against Germany for the expense of the army of occupation of over $255,000,000. Besides this, the Mixed Claims Commission have before them about 12,500 claims of American citizens, aggregating about $1,225,000,000. These claims have already been reduced by a recent decision, but there are valid claims reaching well toward $500,000,000. Our thousands of citizens with credits due them of hundreds of millions of dollars have no redress save in the action of our Government. These are very substantial interests, which it is the duty of our Government to protect as best it can. That course I propose to pursue.

It is for these reasons that we have a direct interest in the economic recovery of Europe. They are enlarged by our desire for the stability of civilization and the welfare of humanity. That we are making sacrifices to that end none can deny. Our deferred interest alone amounts to a million dollars every day. But recently we offered to aid with our advice and counsel. We have reiterated our desire to see France paid and Germany revived. We have proposed disarmament. We have earnestly sought to compose differences and restore peace. We shall persevere in well-doing, not by force, but by reason. . . .

FOREIGN SERVICE

The foreign service of our Government needs to be reorganized and improved.

FISCAL CONDITION

Our main problems are domestic problems. Financial stability is the first requisite of sound government. We can not escape the effect of world conditions. We can not avoid the inevitable results of the economic disorders which have reached all nations. But we shall diminish their harm to us in proportion as we continue to restore our Government finances to a secure and endurable position. This we can and must do. Upon that firm foundation rests the only hope of progress and prosperity. From that source must come relief for the people.

This is being accomplished by a drastic but orderly retrenchment which is bringing our expenses within our means. The origin of this has been the determiniation of the American people, the main support has been the courage of those in authority, and the effective method has been the Budget System. The result has involved real sacrifice by department heads, but it has been made without flinching. This system is a law of the Congress. It represents your will. It must be maintained, and ought to be strengthened by the example of your observance. Without a Budget System there can be no fixed responsibility and no constructive scientific economy.

This great concentration of effort by the administration and Congress has brought the expenditures, exclusive of the self-supporting Post Office Department, down to three billion dollars. It is possible, in consequence, to make a large reduction in the taxes of the people, which is the sole object of all curtailment. This is treated at greater length in the Budget message, and a proposed plan has been presented in detail in a statement by the Secretary of the Treasury which has my unqualified approval. I especially commend a decrease on earned incomes, and further abolition of admission, message, and nuisance taxes. The amusement and educational value of moving pictures ought not to be taxed. Diminishing charges against moderate incomes from investment will afford immense relief, while a revision of the surtaxes will not only provide additional money for capital investment, thus stimulating industry and employing more labor, but will not greatly reduce the revenue from that source, and may in the future actually increase it.

Being opposed to war taxes in time of peace, I am not in favor of excess-profits taxes. A very great service could be rendered through immediate enactment of legislation relieving the people of some of the burden of taxation. To reduce war taxes is to give every home a better chance.

For seven years the people have borne with uncomplaining courage the tremendous burden of national and local taxation. These must both be reduced. The taxes of the Nation must be reduced now as much as prudence will permit, and expenditures must be reduced accordingly. High taxes reach everywhere and burden everybody. They bear most heavily upon the poor. They diminish industry and commerce. They make agriculture unprofitable. They increase the rates on transportation. They are a charge on every necessary of life. Of all services which the Congress can render to the country, I have no hesitation in declaring this one to be paramount. . . .

Another reform which is urgent in our fiscal system is the abolition of the right to issue tax-exempt securities. The existing system not only permits a large amount of the wealth of the Nation to escape its just burden but acts as a continual stimulant to municipal extravagance. This should be prohibited by constitutional amendment. All the wealth of the Nation ought to contribute its fair share to the expenses of the Nation.

TARIFF LAW

The present tariff law has accomplished its two main objects. It has secured an abundant revenue and been productive of an abounding prosperity. Under it the country has had a very large export and import trade. A constant revision of the tariff by the Congress is disturbing and harmful. The present law contains an elastic provision authorizing the President to increase or decrease present schedules not in excess of 50 per centum to meet the difference in cost of production at home and abroad. This does not, to my mind, warrant a rewriting of the whole law, but does mean, and will be so administered, that whenever the required investigation shows that inequalities of sufficient importance exist in any schedule, the power to change them should and will be applied.

SHIPPING

The entire well being of our country is dependent upon transportation by sea and land. Our Government during the war acquired a large merchant fleet which should be transferred, as soon as possible, to private ownership and operation under conditions which would secure two results: First, and of prime importance, adequate means for national defense; second, adequate service to American commerce. Until shipping conditions are such that our fleet can be disposed of advantageously under these conditions, it will be operated as economically as possible under such plans as may be devised from time to time by the Shipping Board. We must have a merchant marine which meets these requirements, and we shall have to pay the cost of its service.

PUBLIC IMPROVEMENTS

The time has come to resume in a moderate way the opening of our intracoastal waterways; the control of flood waters of the Mississippi and of the Colorado Rivers; the improvement of the waterways from the Great Lakes toward the Gulf of Mexico; and the development of the great power and navigation project of the St. Lawrence River, for which efforts are now being made to secure the necessary treaty with Canada. These projects can not all be undertaken at once, but all should have the immediate consideration of the Congress and be adopted as fast as plans can be matured and the necessary funds become available. This is not incompatible with economy, for their nature does not require so much a public expenditure as a capital investment which will be reproductive, as evidenced by the marked increase in revenue from the Panama Canal. Upon these projects depend much future industrial and agricultural progress. They represent the protection of large areas from flood and the addition of a great amount of cheap power and cheap freight by use of navigation, chief of which is the bringing of ocean-going ships to the Great Lakes.

Another problem of allied character is the superpower development of the Northeastern States, consideration of which is proceeding under the direction of the Department of Commerce by joint conference with the local authorities.

RAILROADS

Criticism of the railroad law has been directed, first, to the section laying down the rule by which rates are fixed, and providing for payment to the Government and use of excess earnings; second, to the method for the adjustment of wage scales; and third, to the authority permitting consolidations.

It has been erroneously assumed that the act undertakes to guarantee railroad earnings. The law requires that rates should be just and reasonable. That has always been the rule under which rates have been fixed. To make a rate that does not yield a fair return results in confiscation, and confiscatory rates are of course unconstitutional. Unless the Government adheres to the rule of making a rate that will yield a fair return, it must abandon rate making altogether. The new and important feature of that part of the law is the recapture and redistribution of excess rates. The constitutionality of this method is now before the Supreme Court for adjudication. Their decision should be awaited before attempting further legislation on this subject. Furthermore, the importance of this feature will not be great if consolidation goes into effect.

The settlement of railroad labor disputes is a matter of grave public concern. The Labor Board was established to protect the public in the enjoyment of continuous service by attempting to insure justice between the companies and their employees. It has been a great help, but is not altogether satisfactory to the public, the employees, or the companies. If a substantial agreement can be reached among the groups interested, there should be no hesitation in enacting such agreement into law. If it is not reached, the Labor Board may very well be left for the present to protect the public welfare.

The law for consolidations is not sufficiently effective to be expeditious. Additional legislation is needed giving authority for voluntary consolidations, both regional and route, and providing Government machinery to aid and stimulate such action, always subject to the approval of the Interstate Commerce Commission. This should authorize the commission to appoint committees for each proposed group, representing the public and the component roads, with power to negotiate with individual security holders for an exchange of their securities for those of the consolidation on such terms and conditions as the commission may prescribe for avoiding any confiscation and preserving fair values. Should this permissive consolidation prove ineffective after a limited period, the authority of the Government will have to be directly invoked.

Consolidation appears to be the only feasible method for the maintenance of an adequate system of transportation with an opportunity so to adjust freight rates as to meet such temporary conditions as now prevail in some agricultural sections. Competent authorities agree that an entire reorganization of the rate structure for freight is necessary. This should be ordered at once by the Congress.

DEPARTMENT OF JUSTICE

As no revision of the laws of the United States has been made since 1878, a commission or committee should be created to undertake this work. . . .

It is desirable to expedite the hearing and disposal of cases. A commission of Federal judges and lawyers should be created to recommend legislation by which the procedure in the Federal trial courts may be simplified and regulated by rules of court, rather than by statute; such rules to be submitted to the Congress and to be in force until annulled or modified by the Congress. The Supreme Court needs legislation revising and simplifying the laws governing review by that court, and enlarging the classes of cases of too little public importance to be subject to review. Such reforms would expedite the transaction of the business of the courts. The administration of justice is likely to fail if it be long delayed.

The National Government has never given adequate attention to its prison problems. It ought to provide employment in such form of production as can be used by the Government, though not sold to the public in competition with private business, for all prisoners who can be placed at work, and for which they should receive a reasonable compensation, available for their dependents. . . .

The administration of justice would be facilitated greatly by including in the Bureau of Investigation of the Department of Justice a Division of Criminal Identification, where there would be collected this information which is now indispensable in the suppression of crime.

PROHIBITION

The prohibition amendment to the Constitution requires the Congress and the President to provide adequate laws to prevent its violation. It is my duty to enforce such laws. For that purpose a treaty is being negotiated with Great Britain with respect to the right of search of hovering vessels. To prevent smuggling, the Coast Guard should be greatly strengthened, and a supply of swift power boats should be provided. The major sources of production should be rigidly regulated, and every effort should be made to suppress interstate traffic. With this action on the part of the National Goverment, and the cooperation which is usually rendered by municipal and State authorities, prohibition should be made effective. Free government has no greater menace than disrespect for authority and continual violation of law. It is the duty of a citizen not only to observe the law but to let it be known that he is opposed to its violation.

THE NEGRO

Numbered among our population are some 12,000,000 colored people. Under our Constitution their rights are just as sacred as those of any other citizen. It is both a public and a private duty to protect those rights. The Congress ought to exercise all its powers of prevention and punishment against the hideous crime of lynching, of which the negroes are by no means the sole sufferers, but for which they furnish a majority of the victims.

Already a considerable sum is appropriated to give the negroes vocational training in agriculture. About half a million dollars is recommended for medical courses at Howard University to help contribute to the education of 500 colored doctors needed each year. On account of the migration of large numbers into industrial centers, it has been proposed that a commission be created, composed of members from both races, to formulate a better policy for mutual understanding and confidence. Such an effort is to be commended. Everyone would rejoice in the accomplishment of the results which it seeks. But it is well to recognize that these difficulties are to a large extent local problems which must be worked out by the mutual forbearance and human kindness of each community. Such a method gives much more promise of a real remedy than outside interference.

CIVIL SERVICE

The maintenance and extension of the classified civil service is exceedingly important. There are nearly 550,000 persons in the executive civil service drawing about $700,000,000 of yearly compensation. Four-fifths of these are in the classified service. This method of selection of the employees of the United States is especially desirable for the Post Office Department. The Civil Service Commission has recommended that postmasters at first, second, and third class offices be classified. Such action, accompanied by a repeal of the four-year term of office, would undoubtedly be an improvement. I also recommend that the field force for prohibition enforcement be brought within the classified civil service without covering in the present membership. The best method for selecting public servants is the merit system. . . .

REGULATORY LEGISLATION

Cooperation with other maritime powers is necessary for complete protection of our coast waters from pollution. Plans for this are under way, but await certain experiments for refuse disposal. Meantime laws prohibiting spreading oil and oil refuse from vessels in our own territorial waters would be most helpful against this menace and should be speedily enacted.

Laws should be passed regulating aviation.

Revision is needed of the laws regulating radio interference.

Legislation and regulations establishing load lines to provide safe loading of vessels leaving our ports are necessary and recodification of our navigation laws is vital.

Revision of procedure of the Federal Trade Commission will give more constructive purpose to this department.

If our Alaskan fisheries are to be saved from destruction, there must be further legislation declaring a general policy and delegating the authority to make rules and regulations to an administrative body.

ARMY AND NAVY

For several years we have been decreasing the personnel of the Army and Navy, and reducing their power to the danger point. Further reductions should not be made. The Army is a guarantee of the security of our citizens at home; the Navy is a guarantee of the security of our citizens abroad. Both of these services should be strengthened rather than weakened. Additional planes are needed for the Army, and additional submarines for the Navy. The defenses of Panama must be perfected. We want no more competitive armaments. We want no more war. But we want no weakness that invites imposition. A people who neglect their national defense are putting in jeopardy their national honor. . . .

EDUCATION AND WELFARE

Our National Government is not doing as much as it legitimately can do to promote the welfare of the people. Our enormous material wealth, our institutions, our whole form of society, can not be considered fully successful until their benefits reach the merit of every individual. This not a suggestion that the Government should, or could, assume for the people the inevitable burdens of existence. There is no method by which we can either be relieved of the results of our own folly or be guaranteed a successful life. There is an inescapable personal responsibility for the development of character, of industry, of thrift, and of self-control. These do not come from the Government, but from the people themselves. But the Government can and should always be expressive of steadfast determination, always vigilant, to maintain conditions under which these virtues are most likely to develop and secure recognition and reward. This is the American policy.

It is in accordance with this principle that we have enacted laws for the protection of the public health and have adopted prohibition in narcotic drugs and intoxicating liquors. For purposes of national uniformity we ought to provide, by constitutional amendment and appropriate legislation, for a limitation of child labor and in all cases under the exclusive jurisdiction of the Federal Government a minimum wage law for women, which would undoubtedly find sufficient power of enforcement in the influence of public opinion. . . .

IMMIGRATION

American institutions rest solely on good citizenship. They were created by people who had a background of self-government. New arrivals should be limited to our capacity to absorb them into the ranks of good citizenship. America must be kept American. For this purpose, it is necessary to continue a policy of restricted immigration. It would be well to make such immigration of a selective nature with some inspection at the source, and based either on a prior census or upon the record of naturalization. Either method would insure the admission of those with the largest capacity and best intention of becoming citizens. I am convinced that our present economic and social conditions warrant a limitation of those to be admitted. We should find additional safety in a law requiring the immediate registration of all aliens. Those who do not want to be partakers of the American spirit ought not to settle in America.

VETERANS

No more important duty falls on the Government of the United States than the adequate care of its veterans. Those suffering disabilities incurred in the service must have sufficient hospital relief and compensation. Their dependents must be supported. Rehabilitiation and vocational training must be completed. All of this service must be clean, must be prompt and effective, and it must be administered in a spirit of the broadest and deepest human sympathy. If investigation reveals any present defects of administration or need of legislation, orders will be given for the immediate correction of administration, and recommendations for legislation should be given the highest preference.

At present there are 9,500 vacant beds in Government hospitals. I recommend that all hospitals be authorized at once to receive and care for, without hospital pay, the veterans of all wars needing such care, whenever there are vacant beds, and that immediate steps be taken to enlarge and build new hospitals to serve all such cases.

The American Legion will present to the Congress a legislative program too extensive for detailed discussion here. It is a carefully matured plan. While some of it I do not favor, with much of it I am in hearty accord, and I recommend that a most painstaking effort be made to provide remedies for any defects in the administration of the present laws which their experience has revealed. The attitude of the Government toward these proposals should be one of generosity. But I do not favor the granting of a bonus.

COAL

The cost of coal has become unbearably high. It places a great burden on our industrial and domestic life. The public welfare requires a reduction in the price of fuel. With the enormous deposits in existence, failure of supply ought not to be tolerated. Those responsible for the conditions in this industry should undertake its reform and free it from any charge of profiteering.

The report of the Coal Commission will be before the Congress. It comprises all the facts. It represents the mature deliberations and conclusions of the best talent and experience that ever made a national survey of the production and distribution of fuel. I do not favor Government ownership or operation of coal mines. The need is for action under private ownership that will secure greater continuity of production and greater public protection. The Federal Government probably has no peace-time authority to regulate wages, prices, or profits in coal at the mines or among dealers, but by ascertaining and publishing facts it can exercise great influence.

The source of the difficulty in the bituminous coal fields is the intermittence of operation which causes great waste of both capital and labor. That part of the report dealing with this problem has much significance, and is suggestive of necessary remedies. By amending the car rules, by encouraging greater unity of ownership, and possibly by permitting common selling agents for limited districts on condition that they accept adequate regulations and guarantee that competition between districts be unlimited, distribution, storage, and continuity ought to be improved.

The supply of coal must be constant. In case of its prospective interruption, the President should have authority to appoint a commission empowered to deal with whatever emergency situation might arise, to aid conciliation and voluntary arbitration, to adjust any existing or threatened controversy between the employer and the employee when collective bargaining fails, and by controlling distribution to prevent profiteering in this vital necessity. This legislation is exceedingly urgent, and essential to the exercise of national authority for the protection of the people. Those who undertake the responsibility of management or employment in this industry do so with the full knowledge that the public interest is paramount, and that to fail through any motive of selfishness in its service is such a betrayal of duty as warrants uncompromising action by the Government.

REORGANIZATION

A special joint committee has been appointed to work out a plan for a reorganization of the different departments and bureaus of the Government more scientific and economical than the present system. With the exception of the consolidation of the War and Navy Departments and some minor details, the plan has the general sanction of the President and the Cabinet. It is important that reorganization be enacted into law at the present session.

AGRICULTURE

Aided by the sound principles adopted by the Government, the business of the country has had an extraordinary revival. Looked at as a whole, the Nation is in the enjoyment of remarkable prosperity. Industry and commerce are thriving. For the most part agriculture is successful, eleven staples having risen in value from about $5,300,000,-000 two years ago to about $7,000,000,000 for the current year. But range cattle are still low in price, and some sections of the wheat area, notably Minnesota, North Dakota, and on west, have many cases of actual distress. With his products not selling on a parity with the products of industry, every sound remedy that can be devised should be applied for the relief of the farmer. He represents a character, a type of citizenship, and a public necessity that must be preserved and afforded every facility for regaining prosperity.

The distress is most acute among those wholly dependent upon one crop. Wheat acreage was greatly expanded and has not yet been sufficiently reduced. A large amount is raised for export, which has to meet the competition in the world market of large amounts raised on land much cheaper and much more productive.

No complicated scheme of relief, no plan for Government fixing of prices, no resort to the public Treasury will be of any permanent value in establishing agriculture. Simple and direct methods put into operation by the farmer himself are the only real sources for restoration.

Indirectly the farmer must be relieved by a reduction of national and local taxation. He must be assisted by the reorganization of the freight-rate structure which could reduce charges on his production. To make this fully effective there ought to be railroad consolidations. Cheaper fertilizers must be provided.

He must have organization. His customer with whom he exchanges products of the farm for those of industry is organized, labor is organized, business is organized, and there is no way for agriculture to meet this unless it, too, is organized. The acreage of wheat is too large. Unless we can meet the world market at a profit, we must stop raising for export. Organization would help to reduce acreage. Systems of cooperative marketing created by the farmers themselves, supervised by competent management, without doubt would be of assistance, but they can not wholly solve the problem. Our agricultural schools ought to have thorough courses in the theory of organization and cooperative marketing.

Diversification is necessary. Those farmers who raise their living on their land are not greatly in distress. Such loans as are wisely needed to assist buying stock and other materials to start in this direction should be financed through a Government agency as a temporary and emergency expedient.

The remaining difficulty is the disposition of exportable wheat. I do not favor the permanent interference of the Government in this problem. That probably would increase the trouble by increasing production. But it seems feasible to provide Government assistance to exports, and authority should be given the War Finance Corporation to grant, in its discretion, the most liberal terms of payment for fats and grains exported for the direct benefit of the farm.

MUSCLE SHOALS

The Government is undertaking to develop a great water-power project known as Muscle Shoals, on which it has expended many million dollars. The work is still going on. Subject to the right to retake in time of war, I recommend that this property with a location for auxiliary steam plant and rights of way be sold. This would end the present burden of expense and should return to the Treasury the largest price possible to secure.

While the price is an important element, there is another consideration even more compelling. The agriculture of the Nation needs a greater supply and lower cost of fertilizer. This is now imported in large quantities. The best information I can secure indicates that present methods of power production would not be able profitably to meet the price at which these imports can be sold. To obtain a supply from this water power would require long and costly experimentation to perfect a process for cheap production. Otherwise our purpose would fail completely. It seems desirable, therefore, in order to protect and promote the public welfare, to have adequate covenants that such experimentation be made and carried on to success. The great advantage of low-priced nitrates must be secured for the direct benefit of the farmers and the indirect benefit of the public in time of peace, and of the Government in time of war. If this main object be accomplished, the amount of money received for the property is not a primary or major consideration. . . .

RECLAMATION

By reason of many contributing causes, occupants of our reclamation projects are in financial difficulties, which in some cases are acute. Relief should be granted by definite authority of law empowering the Secretary of the Interior in his discretion to suspend, readjust, and reassess all charges against water users. This whole question is being considered by experts. You will have the advantage of the facts and conclusions which they may develop. This situation, involving a Government investment of more than $135,000,000, and affecting more than 30,000 water users, is serious. While relief which is necessary should be granted, yet contracts with the Government which can be met should be met. The established general policy of these projects should not be abandoned for any private control.

HIGHWAYS AND FORESTS

Highways and reforestation should continue to have the interest and support of the Government. Everyone is anxious for good highways. I have made a liberal proposal in the Budget for the continuing payment to the States by the Federal Government of its share for this necessary public improvement. No expenditure of public money contributes so much to the national wealth as for building good roads.

Reforestation has an importance far above the attention it usually secures. A special committee of the Senate is investigating this need, and I shall welcome a constructive policy based on their report.

It is 100 years since our country announced the Monroe doctrine. This principle has been ever since, and is now, one of the main foundations of our foreign relations. It must be maintained. But in maintaining it we must not be forgetful that a great change has taken place. We are no longer a weak Nation, thinking mainly of defense, dreading foreign imposition. We are great and powerful. New powers bring new responsibilities. Our duty then was to protect ourselves. Added to that, our duty now is to help give stability to the world. We want idealism. We want that vision which lifts men and nations above themselves. These are virtues by reason of their own merit. But they must not be cloistered; they must not be impractical; they must not be ineffective.

The world has had enough of the curse of hatred and selfishness, of destruction and war. It has had enough of the wrongful use of material power. For the healing of the nations there must be good will and charity, confidence and peace. The time has come for a more practical use of moral power, and more reliance upon the principle that right makes its own might. Our authority among the nations must be represented by justice and mercy. It is necessary not only to have faith, but to make sacrifices for our faith. The spiritual forces of the world make all its final determinations. It is with these voices that America should speak. Whenever they declare a righteous purpose there need be no doubt that they will be heard. America has taken her place in the world as a Republic — free, independent, powerful. The best service that can be rendered to humanity is the assurance that this place will be maintained.

SECOND ANNUAL MESSAGE
December 3, 1924

Although President Coolidge looked with favor upon such international efforts as the International Court, further armament reductions and outlawing of war, he made it clear that he felt the country should not get involved in the League of Nations or the political quarrels of other countries. He stressed a reduction of both governmental costs and taxes.

To the Congress of the United States:

The present state of the Union, upon which it is customary for the President to report to the Congress under the provisions of the Constitution, is such that it may be regarded with encouragement and satisfaction by every American. Our country is almost unique in its ability to discharge fully and promptly all its obligations at home and abroad, and provide for all its inhabitants an increase in material resources, in intellectual vigor and in moral power. The Nation holds a position unsurpassed in all former human experience. This does not mean that we do not have any problems. It is elementary that the increasing breadth of our experience necessarily increases the problems of our national life. But it does mean that if we will but apply ourselves industriously and honestly, we have ample powers with which to meet our problems and provide for their speedy solution. I do not profess that we can secure an era of perfection in human existence, but we can provide an era of peace and prosperity, attended with freedom and justice and made more and more satisfying by the ministrations of the charities and humanities of life.

Our domestic problems are for the most part economic. We have our enormous debt to pay, and we are paying it. We have the high cost of government to diminish, and we are diminishing it. We have a heavy burden of taxation to reduce, and we are reducing it. But while remarkable progress has been made in these directions, the work is yet far from accomplished. We still owe over $21,000,000,000, the cost of the National Government is still about $3,500,000,000, and the national taxes still amount to about $27 for each one of our inhabitants. There yet exists this enormous field for the application of economy.

In my opinion the Government can do more to remedy the economic ills of the people by a system of rigid economy in public expenditure than can be accomplished through any other action. The costs of our national and local governments combined now stand at a sum close to $100 for each inhabitant of the land. A little less than one-third of this is represented by national expenditure, and a little more than two-thirds by local expenditure. It is an ominous fact that only the National Government is reducing its debt. Others are increasing theirs at about $1,000,000,000 each year. The depression that overtook business, the disaster experienced in agriculture, the lack of employment and the terrific shrinkage in all values which our country experienced in a most acute form in 1920, resulted in no small measure from the prohibitive taxes which were then levied on all productive effort. The establishment of a system of drastic economy in public expenditure, which has enabled us to pay off about one-fifth of the national debt since 1919, and almost cut in two the national tax burden since 1921, has been one of the main causes in reestablishing a prosperity which has come to include within its benefits almost every one of our inhabitants. Economy reaches everywhere. It carries a blessing to everybody.

The fallacy of the claim that the costs of government are borne by the rich and those who make a direct contribution to the National Treasury can not be too often exposed. No system has been devised, I do not think any system could be devised, under which any person living in this country could escape being affected by the cost of our government. It has a direct effect both upon the rate and the purchasing power of wages. It is felt in the price of those prime necessities of existence, food, clothing, fuel and shelter. It would appear to be elementary that the more the Government expends the more it must require every producer to contribute out of his production to the Public Treasury, and the less he will have for his own benefit. The continuing costs of public administration can be met in only one way — by the work of the people. The higher they become, the more the people must work for the Government. The less they are, the more the people can work for themselves.

The present estimated margin between public receipts and expenditures for this fiscal year is very small. Perhaps the most important work that this session of the Congress can do is to continue a policy of economy and further reduce the cost of government, in order that we may have a reduction of taxes for the next fiscal year. Nothing is more likely to produce that public confidence which is the forerunner and the mainstay of prosperity, encourage and enlarge business opportunity with ample opportunity for employment at good wages, provide a larger market for agricultural products, and put our country in a stronger position to be able to meet the world competition in trade, than a continuing policy of economy. . . .

TAXES

Everyone desires a reduction of taxes, and there is a great preponderance of sentiment in favor of taxation reform. When I approved the present tax law, I stated publicly that I did so in spite of certain provisions which I believed unwise and harmful. One of the most glaring of these was the making public of the amounts assessed against different income-tax payers. Although that damage has now been done, I believe its continuation to be detrimental to the public welfare and bound to decrease public revenues, so that it ought to be repealed.

Anybody can reduce taxes, but it is not so easy to stand in the gap and resist the passage of increasing appropriation bills which would make tax reduction possible. It will be very easy to measure the strength of the attachment to reduced taxation by the power with which increased appropriations are resisted. If at the close of the present session the Congress has kept within the budget which I propose to present, it will then be possible to have a moderate amount of tax reduction and all the tax reform that the Congress may wish for during the next fiscal year. The country is now feeling the direct stimulus which came from the passage of the last revenue bill, and under the assurance of a reasonable system of taxation there is every prospect of an era of prosperity of unprecedented proportions. But it would be idle to expect any such results unless business can continue free from excess profits taxation and be accorded a system of surtaxes at rates which have for their object not the punishment of success or the discouragement of business, but the production of the greatest amount of revenue from large incomes. I am convinced that the larger incomes of the country would actually yield more revenue to the Government if the basis of taxation were scientifically revised downward. Moreover the effect of the present method of this taxation is to increase the cost of interest on productive enterprise and to increase the burden of rent. It is altogether likely that such reduction would so encourage and stimulate investment that it would firmly establish our country in the economic leadership of the world.

WATERWAYS

Meantime our internal development should go on. Provision should be made for flood control of such rivers as the Mississippi and the Colorado, and for the opening up of our inland waterways to commerce. Consideration is due to the project of better navigation from the Great Lakes to the Gulf. Every effort is being made to promote an agreement with Canada to build the St. Lawrence waterway. There are pending before the Congress bills for further development of the Mississippi Basin, for the taking over of the Cape Cod Canal in accordance with a moral obligation which seems to have been incurred during the war, and for the improvement of harbors on both the Pacific and the Atlantic coasts. . . .

RECLAMATION

Our country has a well-defined policy of reclamation established under statutory authority. This policy should be continued and made a self-sustaining activity administered in a manner that will meet local requirements and bring our arid lands into a profitable state of cultivation as fast as there is a market for their products. . . .

No more important development has taken place in the last year than the beginning of a restoration of agriculture to a prosperous condition. We must permit no division of classes in this country, with one occupation striving to secure advantage over another. Each must proceed under open opportunities and with a fair prospect of economic equality. The Government can not successfully insure prosperity or fix prices by legislative fiat. Every business has its risk and its times of depression. It is well known that in the long run there will be a more even prosperity and a more satisfactory range of prices under the natural working out of economic laws than when the Government undertakes the artificial support of markets and industries. Still we can so order our affairs, so protect our own people from foreign competition, so arrange our national finances, so administer our monetary system, so provide for the extension of credits, so improve methods of distribution, as to provide a better working machinery for the transaction of the business of the Nation with the least possible friction and loss. . .

It is estimated that the value of the crops for this harvest year may reach $13,000,000,000, which is an increase of over $3,000,000,000 in three years. It compares with $7,100,000,000 in 1913, and if we make deduction from the figures of 1924 for the comparatively decreased value of the dollar, the yield this year still exceeds 1913 in purchasing power by over $1,000,000,000, and in this interval there has been no increase in the number of farmers. Mostly by his own effort the farmer has decreased the cost of production. A marked increase in the price of his products and some decrease in the price of his supplies has brought him about to a parity with the rest of the Nation. The crop area of this season is estimated at 370,000,000 acres, which is a decline of 3,000,000 acres from last year, and 6,000,000 acres from 1919. This has been a normal and natural application of economic laws, which has placed agriculture on a foundation which is undeniably sound and beginning to be satisfactory. . . .

It was on account of past depression, and in spite of present more encouraging conditions, that I have assembled an Agricultural Conference made up of those who are representative of this great industry in both its operating and economic sides. Everyone knows that the great need of the farmer is markets. The country is not suffering on the side of production. Almost the entire difficulty is on the side of distribution. . . . In time for action at this session, I hope to report to the Congress such legislative remedies as the conference may recommend. . . .

MUSCLE SHOALS

The production of nitrogen for plant food in peace and explosives in war is more and more important. It is one of the chief sustaining elements of life. It is estimated that soil exhaustion each year is represented by about 9,000,000 tons and replenishment by 5,450,000 tons. The deficit of 3,550,000 tons is reported to represent the impairment of 118,000,000 acres of farm lands each year.

To meet these necessities the Government has been developing a water power project at Muscle Shoals to be equipped to produce nitrogen for explosives and fertilizer. It is my opinion that the support of agriculture is the chief problem to consider in connection with this property. It could by no means supply the present needs for nitrogen, but it would help and its development would encourage bringing other water powers into like use.

Several offers have been made for the purchase of this property. Probably none of them represent final terms. Much costly experimentation is necessary to produce commercial nitrogen. For that reason it is a field better suited to private enterprise than to Government operation. I should favor a sale of this property, or long-time lease, under rigid guaranties of commercial nitrogen production at reasonable prices for agricultural use. . . .

RAILWAYS

The railways during the past year have made still further progress in recuperation from the war, with large gains in efficiency and ability expeditiously to handle the traffic of the country. We have now passed through several periods of peak traffic without the car shortages which so frequently in the past have brought havoc to our agriculture and industries. The condition of many of our great freight terminals is still one of difficulty and results in imposing large costs on the public for inward-bound freight, and on the railways for outward-bound freight. Owing to the growth of our large cities and the great increase in the volume of traffic, particularly in perishables, the problem is not only difficult of solution, but in some cases not wholly solvable by railway action alone.

In my message last year I emphasized the necessity for further legislation with a view to expediting the consolidation of our railways into larger systems. The principle of Government control of rates and profits, now thoroughly imbedded in our governmental attitude toward natural monopolies such as the railways, at once eliminates the need of competition by small units as a method of rate adjustment. Competition must be preserved as a stimulus to service, but this will exist and can be increased under enlarged systems. Consequently the consolidation of the railways into larger units for the purpose of securing the substantial values to the public which will come from larger operation has been the logical conclusion of Congress in its previous enactments, and is also supported by the best opinion in the country. . . .

Another matter before the Congress is legislation affecting the labor sections of the transportation act. Much criticism has been directed at the workings of this section and experience has shown that some useful amendment could be made to these provisions.

It would be helpful if a plan could be adopted which, while retaining the practice of systematic collective bargaining with conciliation and voluntary arbitration of labor differences, could also provide simplicity in relations and more direct local responsibility of employees and managers. But such legislation will not meet the requirements of the situation unless it recognizes the principle that the public has a right to the uninterrupted service of transportation, and therefore a right to be heard when there is danger that the Nation may suffer great injury through the interruption of operations because of labor disputes. . . .

SHIPPING BOARD

The form of the organization of the Shipping Board was based originally on its functions as a semijudicial body in regulation of rates. During the war it was loaded with enormous administrative duties. It has been demonstrated time and again that this form of organization results in indecision, division of opinion and administrative functions, which make a wholly inadequate foundation for the conduct of a great business enterprise. The first principle in securing the objective set out by Congress in building up the American merchant marine upon the great trade routes and subsequently disposing of it into private operation can not proceed with effectiveness until the entire functions of the board are reorganized. The immediate requirement is to transfer into the Emergency Fleet Corporation the whole responsibility of operation of the fleet and other property, leaving to the Shipping Board solely the duty of determining certain major policies which require deliberative action. . . .

NATIONAL ELECTIONS

Nothing is so fundamental to the integrity of a republican form of government as honesty in all that relates to the conduct of elections. I am of the opinion that the national laws governing the choice of members of the Congress should be extended to include appropriate representation of the respective parties at the ballot box and equality of representation on the various registration boards, wherever they exist.

THE JUDICIARY

The docket of the Supreme Court is becoming congested. At the opening term last year it had 592 cases, while this year it had 687 cases. Justice long delayed is justice refused. Unless the court be given power by preliminary and summary consideration to determine the importance of cases, and by disposing of those which are not of public moment reserve its time for the more extended consideration of the remainder, the congestion of the docket is likely to increase. It is also desirable that the Supreme Court should have power to improve and reform procedure in suits at law in the Federal courts through the adoption of appropriate rules. The Judiciary Committee of the Senate has reported favorably upon two bills providing for these reforms which should have the immediate favorable consideration of the Congress.

I further recommend that provision be made for the appointment of a commission, to consist of two or three members of the Federal judiciary and as many members of the bar, to examine the present criminal code of procedure and recommend to the Congress measures which may reform and expedite court procedure in the administration and enforcement of our criminal laws.

PRISON REFORM

Pending before the Congress is a bill which has already passed one House providing for a reformatory to which could be committed first offenders and young men for the purpose of segregating them from contact with hardened criminals and providing them with special training, in order to reestablish in them the power to pursue a law-abiding existence in the social and economic life of the Nation. This is a matter of so much importance as to warrant the early attention of the present session. Further provision should also be made, for a like reason, for a separate reformatory for women.

NATIONAL POLICE BUREAU

Representatives of the International Police Conference will bring to the attention of the Congress a proposal for the establishment of a national police bureau. Such action would provide a central point for gathering, compiling, and later distributing to local police authorities much information which would be helpful in the prevention and detection of crime. I believe this bureau is needed, and I recommend favorable consideration of this proposal. . . .

THE WAGE EARNER

Two very important policies have been adopted by this country which, while extending their benefits also in other directions, have been of the utmost importance to the wage earners. One of these is the protective tariff, which enables our people to live according to a better standard and receive a better rate of compensation than any people, any time, anywhere on earth, ever enjoyed. This saves the American market for the products of the American workmen. The other is a policy of more recent origin and seeks to shield our wage earners from the disastrous competition of a great influx of foreign peoples. This has been done by the restrictive immigration law. This saves the American job for the American workmen. I should like to see the administrative features of this law rendered a little more humane for the purpose of permitting those already here a greater latitude in securing admission of members of their own families. But I believe this law in principle is necessary and sound, and destined to increase greatly the public welfare. We must maintain our own economic position, we must defend our own national integrity.

It is gratifying to report that the progress of industry, the enormous increase in individual productivity through labor-saving devices, and the high rate of wages have all combined to furnish our people in general with such an abundance not only of the necessaries but of the conveniences of life that we are by a natural evolution solving our problems of economic and social justice.

THE NEGRO

These developments have brought about a very remarkable improvement in the condition of the negro race. Gradually, but surely, with the almost universal sympathy of those among whom they live, the colored people are working out their own destiny. I firmly believe that it is better for all concerned that they should be cheerfully accorded their full constitutional rights, that they should be protected from all of those impositions to which, from their position, they naturally fall a prey, especially from the crime of lynching, and that they should receive every encouragement to become full partakers in all the blessings of our common American citizenship.

CIVIL SERVICE

The merit system has long been recognized as the correct basis for employment in our civil service. I believe that first, second, and third class postmasters, and without covering in the present membership the field force of prohibition enforcement, should be brought within the classified service by statute law. Otherwise the Executive order of one administration is changed by the Executive order of another administration, and little real progress is made. Whatever its defects, the merit system is certainly to be preferred to the spoils system.

DEPARTMENTAL REORGANIZATION

One way to save public money would be to pass the pending bill for the reorganization of the various departments. . . . Legal authority for a thorough reorganization of the Federal structure with some latitude of action to the Executive in the rearrangement of secondary functions would make for continuing economy in the shift of Government activities which must follow every change in a developing country. . . .

ARMY AND NAVY

Little has developed in relation to our national defense which needs special attention. Progress is constantly being made in air navigation and requires encouragement and development. . . .

Under the limitation of armaments treaty a large saving in outlay and a considerable decrease in maintenance of the Navy has been accomplished. We should maintain the policy of constantly working toward the full treaty strength of the Navy. . . . A special commission also is investigating the problem of petroleum oil for the Navy, considering the best policy to insure the future supply of fuel oil and prevent the threatened drainage of naval oil reserves. . . .

We have been constantly besought to engage in competitive armaments. Frequent reports will reach us of the magnitude of the military equipment of other nations. We shall do well to be little impressed by such reports or such actions. Any nation undertaking to maintain a military establishment with aggressive and imperialistic designs will find itself severely handicapped in the economic development of the world. I believe thoroughly in the Army and Navy, in adequate defense and preparation. But I am opposed to any policy of competition in building and maintaining land or sea armaments.

Our country has definitely relinquished the old standard of dealing with other countries by terror and force, and is definitely committed to the new standard of dealing with them through friendship and understanding. . . . I want the armed forces of America to be considered by all peoples not as enemies but as friends, as the contribution which is made by this country for the maintenance of the peace and security of the world.

VETERANS

With the authorization for general hospitalization of the veterans of all wars provided during the present year, the care and treatment of those who have served their country in time of peril and the attitude of the Government toward them is not now so much one of needed legislation as one of careful, generous and humane administration. It will ever be recognized that their welfare is of the first concern and always entitled to the most solicitous consideration on the part of their fellow citizens. . . .

FOREIGN RELATIONS

At no period in the past 12 years have our foreign relations been in such a satisfactory condition as they are at the present time. Our actions in the recents months have greatly strengthened the American policy of permanent peace with independence. The attitude which our Government took and maintained toward an adjustment of European reparations, by pointing out that it was not a political but a business problem, has demonstrated its wisdom by its actual results. We desire to see Europe restored that it may resume its productivity in the increase of industry and its support in the advance of civilization. We look with great gratification at the hopeful prospect of recuperation in Europe through the Dawes plan. Such assistance as can be given through the action of the public authorities and of our private citizens, through friendly counsel and cooperation, and through economic and financial support, not for any warlike effort but for reproductive enterprise, not to provide means for unsound government financing but to establish sound business administration, should be unhesitatingly provided.

Ultimately nations, like individuals, can not depend upon each other but must depend upon themselves. Each one must work out its own salvation. We have every desire to help. But with all our resources we are powerless to save unless our efforts meet with a constructive response. The situation in our own country and all over the world is one that can be improved only by hard work and self-denial. It is necessary to reduce expenditures, increase savings and liquidate debts. It is in this direction that there lies the greatest hope of domestic tranquillity and international peace. . . .

It is not necessary to stress the general desire of all the people of this country for the promotion of peace. It is the leading principle of all foreign relations. . . . But we do not wish to become involved in the political controversies of others. Nor is the country disposed to become a member of the League of Nations or to assume the obligations imposed by its covenant.

INTERNATIONAL COURT

America has been one of the foremost nations in advocating tribunals for the settlement of international disputes of a justiciable character. Our representatives took a leading part in those conferences which resulted in the establishment of the The Hague Tribunal, and later in providing for a Permanent Court of International Justice. I believe it would be for the advantage of this country and helpful to the stability of other nations for us to adhere to the protocol establishing that court upon the conditions stated in the recommendation which is now before the Senate, and further that our country shall not be bound by advisory opinions which may be rendered by the court upon questions which we have not voluntarily submitted for its judgment. This court would provide a practical and convenient tribunal before which we could go voluntarily, but to which we could not be summoned, for a determination of justiciable questions when they fail to be resolved by diplomatic negotaitions.

DISARMAMENT CONFERENCE

Many times I have expressed my desire to see the work of the Washington Conference on Limitation of Armaments appropriately supplemented by further agreements for a further reduction and for the purpose of diminishing the menace and waste of the competition in preparing instruments of international war. It has been and is my expectation that we might hopefully approach other great powers for further conference on this subject as soon as the carrying out of the present reparation plan as the established and settled policy of Europe has created a favorable opportunity. But on account of proposals which have already been made by other governments for a European conference, it will be necessary to wait to see what the outcome of their actions may be. I should not wish to propose or have representatives attend a conference which would contemplate commitments opposed to the freedom of action we desire to maintain unimpaired with respect to our purely domestic policies.

INTERNATIONAL LAW

Our country should also support efforts which are being made toward the condification of international law. . . .

OUTLAW OF WAR

Much interest has of late been manifested in this country in the discussion of various proposals to outlaw aggressive war. I look with great sympathy upon the examination of this subject. It is in harmony with the traditional policy of our country, which is against aggressive war and for the maintenance of permanent and honorable peace. While, as I have said, we must safeguard our liberty to deal according to our own judgment with our domestic policies, we can not fail to view with sympathetic interest all progress to this desired end or carefully to study the measures that may be proposed to attain it.

LATIN AMERICA

While we are desirous of promoting peace in every quarter of the globe, we have a special interest in the peace of this hemisphere. It is our constant desire that all causes of dispute in this area may be tranquilly and satisfactorily adjusted. Along with our desire for peace is the earnest hope for the increased prosperity of our sister republics of Latin America, and our constant purpose to promote cooperation with them which may be mutually beneficial and always inspired by the most cordial friendships.

FOREIGN DEBTS

About $12,000,000,000 is due to our Government from abroad, mostly from European Governments. Great Britain, Finland, Hungary, Lithuania and Poland have negotiated settlements amounting close to $5,000,000,000. This represents the funding of over 42 per cent of the debt since the creation of the special Foreign Debt Commission. As the life of this commission is about to expire, its term should be extended. I am opposed to the cancellation of these debts and believe it for the best welfare of the world that they should be liquidated and paid as fast as possible. I do not favor oppressive measures, but unless money that is borrowed is repaid credit can not be secured in time of necessity, and there exists besides a moral obligation which our country can not ignore and no other country can evade. Terms and conditions may have to conform to differences in the financial abilities of the countries concerned, but the principle that each country should meet its obligation admits of no differences and is of universal application.

It is axiomatic that our country can not stand still. It would seem to be perfectly plain from recent events that it is determined to go forward. But it wants no pretenses, it wants no vagaries. It is determined to advance in an orderly, sound and common-sense way. It does not propose to abandon the theory of the Declaration that the people have inalienable rights which no majority and no power of government can destroy. It does not propose to abandon the practice of the Constitution that provides for the protection of these rights. It believes that within these limitations, which are imposed not by the fiat of man but by the law of the Creator, self-government is just and wise. It is convinced that it will be impossible for the people to provide their own government unless they continue to own their own property.

These are the very foundations of America. On them has been erected a Government of freedom and equality, of justice and mercy, of education and charity. Living under it and supporting it the people have come into great possessions on the material and spiritual sides of life. I want to continue in this direction. I know that the Congress shares with me that desire. I want our institutions to be more and more expressive of these principles. I want the people of all the earth to see in the American flag the symbol of a Government which intends no oppression at home and no aggression abroad, which in the spirit of a common brotherhood provides assistance in time of distress.

INAUGURAL ADDRESS
March 4, 1925

This speech, expressing great confidence in the country's future, was the first inaugural address to be broadcast over the radio. Its measured pace contrasted strongly to the speech delivered shortly before by Vice President Charles G. Dawes at his induction in the Senate chamber, in which he harshly attacked the practice of filibuster.

My Countrymen:

No one can contemplate current conditions without finding much that is satisfying and still more that is encouraging. Our own country is leading the world in the general readjustment to the results of the great conflict. Many of its burdens will bear heavily upon us for years, and the secondary and indirect effects we must expect to experience for some time. But we are beginning to comprehend more definitely what course should be pursued, what remedies ought to be applied, what actions should be taken for our deliverance, and are clearly manifesting a determined will faithfully and conscientiously to adopt these methods of relief. Already we have sufficiently rearranged our domestic affairs so that confidence has returned, business has revived, and we appear to be entering an era of prosperity which is gradually reaching into every part of the Nation. Realizing that we can not live unto ourselves alone, we have contributed of our resources and our counsel to the relief of the suffering and the settlement of the disputes among the European nations. Because of what America is and what America has done, a firmer courage, a higher hope, inspires the heart of all humanity.

These results have not occurred by mere chance. They have been secured by a constant and enlightened effort marked by many sacrifices and extending over many generations. We can not continue these brilliant successes in the future, unless we continue to learn from the past. It is necessary to keep the former experiences of our country both at home and abroad continually before us, if we are to have any science of government. If we wish to erect new structures, we must have a definite knowledge of the old foundations. We must realize that human nature is about the most constant thing in the universe and that the essentials of human relationship do not change. We must frequently take our bearings from these fixed stars of our political firmament if we expect to hold a true course. If we examine carefully what we have done, we can determine the more accurately what we can do.

We stand at the opening of the one hundred and fiftieth year since our national consciousness first asserted itself by unmistakable action with an array of force. The old sentiment of detached and dependent colonies disappeared in the new sentiment of a united and independent Nation. Men began to discard the narrow confines of a local charter for the broader opportunities of a national constitution. Under the eternal urge of freedom we became an independent Nation. A little less than 50 years later that freedom and independence were reasserted in the face of all the world, and guarded, supported, and secured by the Monroe doctrine. The narrow fringe of States along the Atlantic seaboard advanced its frontiers across the hills and plains of an intervening continent until it passed down the golden slope to the Pacific. We made freedom a birthright. We extended our domain over distant islands in order to safeguard our own interests and accepted the consequent obligation to bestow justice and liberty upon less favored peoples. In the defense of our own ideals and in the general cause of liberty we entered the Great War. When victory had been fully secured, we withdrew to our own shores unrecompensed save in the consciousness of duty done.

Throughout all these experiences we have enlarged our freedom, we have strengthened our independence. We have been, and propose to be, more and more American. We believe that we can best serve our own country and most successfully discharge our obligations to humanity by continuing to be openly and candidly, intensely and scrupulously, American. If we have any heritage, it has been that. If we have any destiny, we have found it in that direction.

But if we wish to continue to be distinctively American, we must continue to make that term comprehensive enough to embrace the legitimate desires of a civilized and enlightened people determined in all their relations to pursue a conscientious and religious life. We can not permit ourselves to be narrowed and dwarfed by slogans and phrases. It is not the adjective, but the substantive, which is of real importance. It is not the name of the action, but the result of the action, which is the chief concern. It will be well not to be too much disturbed by the thought of either isolation or entanglement of pacifists and militarists. The physical configuration of the earth has separated us from all of the Old World, but the common brotherhood of man, the highest law of all our being, has united us by inseparable bonds with all humanity. Our country represents nothing but peaceful intentions toward all the earth, but it ought not to fail to maintain such a military force as comports with the dignity and security of a great people. It ought to be a balanced force, intensely modern, capable of defense by sea and land, beneath the surface and in the air. But it should be so conducted that all the world may see in it, not a menace, but an instrument of security and peace.

This Nation believes thoroughly in an honorable peace under which the rights of its citizens are to be everywhere protected. It has never found that the necessary enjoyment of such a peace could be maintained only by a great and threatening array of arms. In common with other nations, it is now more determined than ever to promote peace through friendliness and good will, through mutual understandings and mutual forbearance. We have never practiced the policy of competitive armaments. We have recently committed ourselves by covenants with the other great nations to a limitation of our sea power. As one result of this, our Navy ranks larger, in comparison, than it ever did before. Removing the burden of expense and jealousy, which must always accrue from a keen rivalry, is one of the most effective methods of diminishing that unreasonable hysteria and misunderstanding which are the most potent means of fomenting war. This policy represents a new departure in the world. It is a thought, an ideal, which has led to an entirely new line of action. It will not be easy to maintain. Some never moved from their old position, some are constantly slipping back to the old ways of thought and the old action of seizing a musket and relying on force. America has taken the lead in this new direction, and that lead America must continue to hold. If we expect others to rely on our fairness and justice we must show that we rely on their fairness and justice.

If we are to judge by past experience, there is much to be hoped for in international relations from frequent conferences and consultations. We have before us the beneficial results of the Washington conference and the various consultations recently held upon European affairs, some of which were in response to our suggestions and in some of which we were active participants. Even the failures can not but be accounted useful and an immeasurable advance over threatened or actual warfare. I am strongly in favor of a continuation of this policy, whenever conditions are such that there is even a promise that practical and favorable results might be secured.

In conformity with the principle that a display of reason rather than a threat of force should be the determining factor in the intercourse among nations, we have long advocated the peaceful settlement of disputes by methods of arbitration and have negotiated many treaties to secure that result. The same considerations should lead to our adherence to the Permanent Court of International Justice. Where great principles are involved, where great movements are under way which promise much for the welfare of humanity by reason of the very fact that many other nations have given such movements their actual support, we ought not to withhold our own sanction because of any small and inessential difference, but only upon the ground of the most important and compelling fundamental reasons. We can not barter away our independence or our sovereignty, but we ought to engage in no refinements of logic, no sophistries, and no subterfuges, to argue away the undoubted duty of this country by reason of the might of its numbers, the power of its resources, and its position of leadership in the world, actively and comprehensively to signify its approval and to bear its full share of the responsibility of a candid and disinterested attempt at the establishment of a tribunal for the administration of even-handed justice between nation and nation. The weight of our enormous influence must be cast upon the side of a reign not of force but of law and trial, not by battle but by reason.

We have never any wish to interfere in the political conditions of any other countries. Especially are we determined not to become implicated in the political controversies of the Old World. With a great deal of hesitation, we have responded to appeals for help to maintain order, protect life and property, and establish responsible government in some of the small countries of the Western Hemisphere. Our private citizens have advanced large sums of money to assist in the necessary financing and relief of the Old World. We have not failed, nor shall we fail to respond, whenever necessary to mitigate human suffering and assist in the rehabilitation of distressed nations. These, too, are requirements which must be met by reason of our vast powers and the place we hold in the world.

Some of the best thought of mankind has long been seeking for a formula for permanent peace. Undoubtedly the clarification of the principles of international law would be helpful, and the efforts of scholars to prepare such a work for adoption by the various nations should have our sympathy and support. Much may be hoped for from the earnest studies of those who advocate the outlawing of aggressive war. But all these plans and preparations, these treaties and covenants, will not of themselves be adequate. One of the greatest dangers to peace lies in the economic pressure to which people find themselves subjected. One of the most practical things to be done in the world is to seek arrangements under which such pressure may be removed, so that opportunity may be renewed and hope may be revived. There must be some assurance that effort and endeavor will be followed by success and prosperity. In the making and financing of such adjustments there is not only an opportunity, but a real duty for America to respond with her counsel and her resources. Conditions must be provided under which people can make a living and work out of their difficulties. But there is another element, more important than all, without which there can not be the slightest hope of a permanent peace. That element lies in the heart of humanity. Unless the desire for peace be cherished there, unless this fundamental and only natural source of brotherly love be cultivated to its highest degree, all artificial efforts will be in vain. Peace will come when there is realization that only under a reign of law, based on righteousness and supported by the religious conviction of the brotherhood of man, can there be any hope of a complete and satisfying life. Parchment will fail, the sword will fail, it is only the spiritual nature of man that can be triumphant.

It seems altogether probable that we can contribute most to these important objects by maintaining our position of political detachment and independence. We are not identified with any Old World interest. This position should be made more and more clear in our relations with all foreign countries. We are at peace with all of them. Our program is never to oppress, but always to assist. But while we do justice to others, we must require that justice be done to us. With us a treaty of peace means peace, and a treaty of amity means amity. We have made great contributions to the settlement of contentious differences in both Europe and Asia. But there is a very definite point beyond which we can not go. We can only help those who help themselves. Mindful of these limitations, the one great duty that stands out requires us to use our enormous powers to trim the balance of the world.

While we can look with a great deal of pleasure upon what we have done abroad, we must remember that our continued success in that direction depends upon what we do at home. Since its very outset, it has been found necessary to conduct our Government by means of political parties. That system would not have survived from generation to generation if it had not been fundamentally sound and provided the best instrumentalities for the most complete expression of the popular will. It is not necessary to claim that it has always worked perfectly. It is enough to know that nothing better has been devised. No one would deny that there should be full and free expression and an opportunity for independence of action within the party. There is no salvation in a narrow and bigoted partisanship. But if there is to be responsible party government, the party label must be something more than a mere device for securing office. Unless those who are elected under the same party designation are willing to assume sufficient responsibility and exhibit sufficient loyalty and coherence, so that they can cooperate with each other in the support of the broad general principles of the party platform, the election is merely a mockery, no decision is made at the polls, and there is no representation of the popular will. Common honesty and good faith with the people who support a party at the polls require that party, when it enters office, to assume the control of that portion of the Government to which it has been elected. Any other course is bad faith and a violation of the party pledges.

When the country has bestowed its confidence upon a party by making it a majority in the Congress, it has a right to expect such unity of action as will make the party majority an effective instrument of government. This administration has come into power with a very clear and definite mandate from the people. The expression of the popular will in favor of maintaining our constitutional guarantees was overwhelming and decisive. There was a manifestation of such faith in the integrity of the courts that we can consider that issue rejected for some time to come. Likewise, the policy of public ownership of railroads and certain electric utilities met with unmistakable defeat. The people declared that they wanted their rights to have not a political but a judicial determination, and their independence and freedom continued and supported by having the ownership and control of their property, not in the Government, but in their own hands. As they always do when they have a fair chance, the people demonstrated that they are sound and are determined to have a sound government.

When we turn from what was rejected to inquire what was accepted, the policy that stands out with the greatest clearness is that of economy in public expenditure with reduction and reform of taxation. The principle involved in this effort is that of conservation. The resources of this country are almost beyond computation. No mind can comprehend them. But the cost of our combined governments is likewise almost beyond definition. Not only those who are now making their tax returns, but those who meet the enhanced cost of existence in their monthly bills, know by hard experience what this great burden is and what it does. No matter what others may want, these people want a drastic economy. They are opposed to waste. They know that extravagance lengthens the hours and diminishes the rewards of their labor. I favor the policy of economy, not because I wish to save money, but because I wish to save people. The men and women of this country who toil are the ones who bear the cost of the Government. Every dollar that we prudently save means that their life will be so much the more abundant. Economy is idealism in its most practical form.

If extravagance were not reflected in taxation, and through taxation both directly and indirectly injuriously affecting the people, it would not be of so much consequence. The wisest and soundest method of solving our tax problem is through economy. Fortunately, of all the great nations this country is best in a position to adopt that simple remedy. We do not any longer need war-time revenues. The collection of any taxes which are not absolutely required, which do not beyond reasonable doubt contribute to the public welfare, is only a species of legalized larceny. Under this Republic the rewards of industry belong to those who earn them. The only constitutional tax is the tax which ministers to public necessity. The property of the country belongs to the people of the country. Their title is absolute. They do not support any privileged class; they do not need to maintain great military forces; they ought not to be burdened with a great array of public employees. They are not required to make any contribution to Government expenditures except that which they voluntarily assess upon themselves through the action of their own representatives. Whenever taxes become burdensome a remedy can be applied by the people; but if they do not act for themselves, no one can be very successful in acting for them.

The time is arriving when we can have further tax reduction, when, unless we wish to hamper the people in their right to earn a living, we must have tax reform. The method of raising revenue ought not to impede the transaction of business; it ought to encourage it. I am opposed to extremely high rates, because they produce little or no revenue, because they are bad for the country, and, finally, because they are wrong. We can not finance the country, we can not improve social conditions, through any system of injustice, even if we attempt to inflict it upon the rich. Those who suffer the most harm will be the poor. This country believes in prosperity. It is absurd to suppose that it is envious of those who are already prosperous. The wise and correct course to follow in taxation and all other economic legislation is not to destroy those who have already secured success but to create conditions under which every one will have a better chance to be successful. The verdict of the country has been given on this question. That verdict stands. We shall do well to heed it.

These questions involve moral issues. We need not concern ourselves much about the rights of property if we will faithfully observe the rights of persons. Under our institutions their rights are supreme. It is not property but the right to hold property, both great and small, which our Constitution guarantees. All owners of property are charged with a service. These rights and duties have been revealed, through the conscience of society, to have a divine sanction. The very stability of our society rests upon production and conservation. For individuals or for governments to waste and squander their resources is to deny these rights and disregard these obligations. The result of economic dissipation to a nation is always moral decay.

These policies of better international understandings, greater economy, and lower taxes have contributed largely to peaceful and prosperous industrial relations. Under the helpful influences of restrictive immigration and a protective tariff, employment is plentiful, the rate of pay is high, and wage earners are in a state of contentment seldom before seen. Our transportation systems have been gradually recovering and have been able to meet all the requirements of the service. Agriculture has been very slow in reviving, but the price of cereals at last indicates that the day of its deliverance is at hand.

We are not without our problems, but our most important problem is not to secure new advantages but to maintain those which we already possess. Our system of government made up of three separate and independent departments, our divided sovereignty composed of Nation and State, the matchless wisdom that is enshrined in our Constitution, all these need constant effort and tireless vigilance for their protection and support.

In a republic the first rule for the guidance of the citizen is obedience to law. Under a despotism the law may be imposed upon the subject. He has no voice in its making, no influence in its administration, it does not represent him. Under a free government the citizen makes his own laws, chooses his own administrators, which do represent him. Those who want their rights respected under the Constitution and the law ought to set the example themselves of observing the Constitution and the law. While there may be those of high intelligence who violate the law at times, the barbarian and the defective always violate it. Those who disregard the rules of society are not exhibiting a superior intelligence, are not promoting freedom and independence, are not following the path of civilization, but are displaying the traits of ignorance, of servitude, of savagery, and treading the way that leads back to the jungle.

The essence of a republic is representative government. Our Congress represents the people and the States. In all legislative affairs it is the natural collaborator with the President. In spite of all the criticism which often falls to its lot, I do not hesitate to say that there is no more independent and effective legislative body in the world. It is, and should be, jealous of its prerogative. I welcome its cooperation, and expect to share with it not only the responsibility, but the credit, for our common effort to secure beneficial legislation.

These are some of the principles which America represents. We have not by any means put them fully into practice, but we have strongly signified our belief in them. The encouraging feature of our country is not that it has reached its destination, but that it has overwhelmingly expressed its determination to proceed in the right direction. It is true that we could, with profit, be less sectional and more national in our thought. It would be well if we could replace much that is only a false and ignorant prejudice with a true and enlightened pride of race. But the last election showed that appeals to class and nationality had little effect. We were all found loyal to a common citizenship. The fundamental precept of liberty is toleration. We can not permit any inquisition either within or without the law or apply any religious test to the holding of office. The mind of America must be forever free.

It is in such contemplations, my fellow countrymen, which are not exhaustive but only representative, that I find ample warrant for satisfaction and encouragement. We should not let the much that is to do obscure the much which has been done. The past and present show faith and hope and courage fully justified. Here stands our country, an example of tranquillity at home, a patron of tranquillity abroad. Here stands its Government, aware of its might but obedient to its conscience. Here it will continue to stand, seeking peace and prosperity, solicitous for the welfare of the wage earner, promoting enterprise, developing waterways and natural resources, attentive to the intuitive counsel of womanhood, encouraging education, desiring the advancement of religion, supporting the cause of justice and honor among the nations. America seeks no earthly empire built on blood and force. No ambition, no temptation, lures her to thought of foreign dominions. The legions which she sends forth are armed, not with the sword, but with the cross. The higher state to which she seeks the allegiance of all mankind is not of human, but of divine origin. She cherishes no purpose save to merit the favor of Almighty God.

CORONADO CO v. U. M. WORKERS
May 25, 1925

The Supreme Court, in the action by Coronado Coal Co. against the United Mine Workers of America, ruled that local unions were guilty of violation of the federal Anti-trust Act by destroying valuable mining properties.

. . . This is a suit for damages for the effect of an alleged conspiracy of the defendants unlawfully to restrain and prevent plaintiff's interstate trade in coal in violation of the first and second sections of the Federal Anti-Trust Act. The charge is that the defendants, in 1914, for the purpose of consummating the conspiracy, destroyed valuable mining properties of the plaintiffs. Treble damages and an attorney's fee are asked under the seventh section of the Act. The suit was brought in the District Court for the Western District of Arkansas. The plaintiffs are the Bache-Denman Coal Company and eight other corporations, in each of which the first named owns a controlling amount of stock. One of them is the Coronado Company, which gives the case its name. The corporations were correlated in organization and in the physical location of their mines. They had been operated for some years as a unit in the Prairie Creek Valley in Sebastian County, Arkansas. . . .

In our previous opinion we held that the International Union, known as the United Mine Workers of America, the union known as United Mine Workers, District No. 21, and the subordinate local unions which were made defendants, were, though unincorporated associations, subject to suit under the Anti-Trust Act, but that there was not sufficient evidence to go to the jury to show participation by the International Union in the conspiracy and the wrongs done. We found evidence tending to show that District No. 21 and other defendants were engaged in the conspiracy and the destruction of the property, but not enough to show an intentional restraint of interstate trade and a violation of the Anti-Trust Act. The plaintiffs contend that they have now supplied the links lacking at the first trial against each of the principal defendants. . . .

In addition to this, the testimony of McNamara, already discussed, while ineffective to establish the complicity of the International Union with this conspiracy, contains much, if credited, from which the jury could reasonably infer that the purpose of the union miners in District No. 21 and the local unions engaged in the plan was to destroy the power of the owners and lessees of the Bache-Denman mines to send their output into interstate commerce to compete with that of union mines in Oklahoma, in Kansas, in Louisiana markets and elsewhere. . . .

New and more elaborate evidence was also introduced in the second trial as to the capacity of the Bache-Denman mines under the open shop. . . .

The mere reduction in the supply of an article to be shipped in interstate commerce by the illegal or tortious prevention of its manufacture or production is ordinarily an indirect and remote obstruction to that commerce. But when the intent of those unlawfully preventing the manufacture or production is shown to be to restrain or control the supply entering and moving in interstate commerce, or the price of it in interstate markets, their action is a direct violation of the Anti-Trust Act. . . . We think there was substantial evidence at the second trial in this case tending to show that the purpose of the destruction of the mines was to stop the production of non-union coal and prevent its shipment to markets of other States than Arkansas, where it would by competition tend to reduce the price of the commodity and affect injuriously the maintenance of wages for union labor in competing mines. . . .

AGNELLO v. UNITED STATES
October 12, 1925

*In this case, the Supreme Court ruled that search of a
home without a warrant was unconstitutional.*

While the question has never been directly decided by this court,
it has always been assumed that one's house cannot lawfully be searched
without a search warrant, except as an incident to a lawful arrest
therein. . . . The protection of the Fourth Amendment extends to all
equally, — to those justly suspected or accused, as well as to the in-
nocent. The search of a private dwelling without a warrant is in itself
unreasonable and abhorrent to our laws. Congress has never passed
an act purporting to authorize the search of a house without a warrant.
On the other hand, special limitations have been set about the obtaining of search warrants for that purpose. . . . Save in certain cases as
incident to arrest, there is no sanction in the decisions of the courts,
federal or state, for the search of a private dwelling house without
a warrant. Absence of any judicial approval is persuasive authority
that it is unlawful. . . . Belief, however well founded, that an article
sought is concealed in a dwelling house furnishes no justification for a
search of that place without a warrant. And such searches are held
unlawful notwithstanding facts unquestionably showing probable
cause. . . . The search of Frank Agnello's house and seizure of the
can of cocaine violated the Fourth Amendment. . . .

THIRD ANNUAL MESSAGE
December 8, 1925

*Coolidge's general theme was one of great prosperity,
with a sidenote of continuing governmental economy.*

Members of the Congress:

In meeting the constitutional requirement of informing the Congress
upon the state of the Union, it is exceedingly gratifying to report that
the general condition is one of progress and prosperity. Here and
there are comparatively small and apparently temporary difficulties
needing adjustment and improved administrative methods, such as are
always to be expected, but in the fundamentals of government and business the results demonstrate that we are going in the right direction.
The country does not appear to require radical departures from the
policies already adopted so much as it needs a further extension of
these policies and the improvement of details. . . . The greatest
solicitude should be exercised to prevent any encroachment upon the
rights of the States or their various political subdivisions. . . .

GOVERNMENT ECONOMY

It is a fundamental principle of our country that the people are
sovereign. While they recognize the undeniable authority of the state,
they have established as its instrument a Government of limited powers.
They hold inviolate in their own hands the jurisdiction over their own
freedom and the ownership of their own property. Neither of these can
be impaired except by due process of law. The wealth of our country
is not public wealth, but private wealth. It does not belong to the Government, it belongs to the people. The Government has no justification
in taking private property except for a public purpose. It is always
necessary to keep these principles in mind in the laying of taxes and
in the making of appropriations. No right exists to levy on a dollar, or
to order the expenditure of a dollar, of the money of the people, except
for a necessary public purpose duly authorized by the Constitution.
The power over the purse is the power over liberty.

That is the legal limitation within which the Congress can act.
How it will proceed within this limitation is always a question of
policy. When the country is prosperous and free from debt, when the
rate of taxation is low, opportunity exists for assuming new burdens
and undertaking new enterprises. Such a condition now prevails only
to a limited extent. All proposals for assuming new obligations ought
to be postponed, unless they are reproductive capital investments or
are such as are absolutely necessary at this time. We still have an

enormous debt of over $20,000,000,000, on which the interest and sinking-fund requirements are $1,320,000,000. Our appropriations for the Pension Office and the Veterans' Bureau are $600,000,000. The War and Navy Departments call for $642,000,000. Other requirements, exclusive of the Post Office, which is virtually self-sustaining, brought the appropriations for the current year up to almost $3,100,000,000. This shows an expenditure of close to $30 for every inhabitant of our country. For the average family of five it means a tax, directly or indirectly paid, of about $150 for national purposes alone. The local tax adds much more. These enormous expenditures ought not to be increased, but through every possible effort they ought to be reduced.

Only one of these great items can be ultimately extinguished. That is the item of our war debt. Already this has been reduced by about $6,000,000,000, which means an annual saving in interest of close to $250,000,000. The present interest charge is about $820,000,000 yearly. It would seem to be obvious that the sooner this debt can be retired the more the taxpayers will save in interest and the easier it will be to secure funds with which to prosecute needed running expenses, constructions, and improvements. This item of $820,000,000 for interest is a heavy charge on all the people of the country, and it seems to me that we might well consider whether it is not greatly worth while to dispense with it as early as possible by retiring the principal debt which it is required to serve.

It has always been our policy to retire our debts. That of the Revolutionary War period, not withstanding the additions made in 1812, was paid by 1835, and the Civil War debt within 23 years. Of the amount already paid, over $1,000,000,000 is a reduction in cash balances. That source is exhausted. Over one and two-thirds billions of dollars was derived from excess receipts. Tax reduction eliminates that. The sale of surplus war materials has been another element of our income. That is practically finished. With these eliminated, the reduction of the debt has been only about $500,000,000 each year, not an excessive sum on so large a debt. . . .

The more we pay while prices are high, the easier it will be.

Deflation of government after a war period is slower than deflation of business, where curtailment is either prompt and effective or disaster follows. There is room for further economy in the cost of the Federal Government, but a comparison of current expenditures with pre-war expenditures is not unfavorable to the efficiency with which Government business is now being done. . . .

This does not mean that further economies will not come. As we reduce our debt our interest charges decline. There are many details yet to correct. The real improvement, however, must come not from additional curtailment of expenses, but by a more intelligent, more ordered spending. Our economy must be constructive. While we should avoid as far as possible increases in permanent current expenditures, oftentimes a capital outlay like internal improvements will result in actual constructive saving. That is economy in its best sense. . . .

A mere policy of economy without any instrumentalities for putting it into operation would be very ineffective. The Congress has wisely set up the Bureau of the Budget to investigate and inform the President what recommendations he ought to make for current appropriations. . . .

But it is evidently not enough to have care in making appropriations without any restraint upon expenditure. The Congress has provided that check by establishing the office of Comptroller General. . . .

The Congress has absolute authority over the appropriations and is free to exercise its judgment as the evidence may warrant, in increasing or decreasing budget recommendations. But it ought to resist every effort to weaken or break down this most beneficial system of supervising appropriations and expenditures. Without it all the claim of economy would be a mere pretense.

TAXATION

The purpose of reducing expenditures is to secure a reduction in taxes. That purpose is about to be realized. With commendable promptness the Ways and Means Committee of the House has undertaken in advance of the meeting of the Congress to frame a revenue act. As the bill has proceeded through the committee it has taken on a nonpartisan character, and both Republicans and Democrats have joined in a measure which embodies many sound principles of tax reform. The bill will correct substantially the economic defects injected into the revenue act of 1924, as well as many which have remained as wartime legacies. In its present form it should provide sufficient revenue for the Government.

The excessive surtaxes have been reduced, estate tax rates are restored to more reasonable figures, with every prospect of withdrawing from the field when the States have had the opportunity to correct the abuses in their own inheritance tax laws, the gift tax and publicity section are to be repealed, many miscellaneous taxes are lowered or abandoned, and the Board of Tax Appeals and the administrative features of the law are improved and strengthened. I approve of the bill in principle. In so far as income-tax exemptions are concerned, it seems to me the committee has gone as far as it is safe to go and somewhat further than I should have gone. Any further extension along these lines would, in my opinion, impair the integrity of our income-tax system.

I am advised that the bill will be through the House by Christmas. For this prompt action the country can thank the good sense of the Ways and Means Committee in framing an economic measure upon economic considerations. If this attitude continues to be reflected through the Congress, the taxpayer will have his relief by the time his March 15 installment of income taxes is due. . . .

FOREIGN RELATIONS

The policy of our foreign relations, casting aside any suggestion of force, rests solely on the foundation of peace, good will, and good works. We have sought, in our intercourse with other nations, better understandings through conference and exchange of views as befits beings endowed with reason. The results have been the gradual elimination of disputes, the settlement of controversies, and the establishment of a firmer friendship between America and the rest of the world than has ever existed at any previous time.

The example of this attitude has not been without its influence upon other countries. Acting upon it, an adjustment was made of the difficult problem of reparations. This was the second step toward peace in Europe. It paved the way for the agreements which were drawn up at the Locarno Conference. When ratified, these will represent the third step toward peace. While they do not of themselves provide an economic rehabilitation, which is necessary for the progress of Europe, by strengthening the guaranties of peace they diminish the need for great armaments. If the energy which now goes into military effort is transferred to productive endeavor, it will greatly assist economic progress.

The Locarno agreements were made by the European countries directly interested without any formal intervention of America, although on July 3 I publicly advocated such agreements in an address made in Massachusetts. We have consistently refrained from intervening except when our help has been sought and we have felt it could be effectively given, as in the settlement of reparations and the London Conference. These recent Locarno agreements represent the success of this policy which we have been insisting ought to be adopted, of having European countries settle their own political problems without involving this country. This beginning seems to demonstrate that this policy is sound. . . .

When these agreements are finally adopted, they will provide guaranties of peace that make the present prime reliance upon force in some parts of Europe very much less necessary. The natural corollary to these treaties should be further international contract for the limitation of armaments. This work was successfully begun at the Washington Conference. Nothing was done at that time concerning land forces because of European objection. Our standing army has been reduced to around 118,000, about the necessary police force for 115,000,000 people. . . .

It seems clear that it is the reduction of armies rather than of navies that is of the first importance to the world at the present time.

We shall look with great satisfaction upon that effort and give it our approbation and encouragement. If that can be settled, we may more easily consider further reduction and limitation of naval armaments. For that purpose our country has constantly through its Executive, and through repeated acts of Congress, indicated its willingness to call such a conference. Under congressional sanction it would seem to be wise to participate in any conference of the great powers for naval limitation of armament proposed upon such conditions that it would hold a fair promise of being effective. . . .

In the further pursuit of strengthening the bonds of peace and good will we have joined with other nations in an international conference held at Geneva and signed an agreement which will be laid before the Senate for ratification providing suitable measures for control and for publicity in international trade in arms, ammunition, and implements of war, and also executed a protocol providing for a prohibition of the use of poison gas in war, in accordance with the principles of Article 5 of the treaty relating thereto signed at the Washington Conference. We are supporting the Pan American efforts that are being made toward the codification of international law, and looking with sympathy on the investigations being conducted under philanthropic auspices of the proposal to make agreements outlawing war. In accordance with promises made at the Washington Conference, we have urged the calling of and are now represented at the Chinese Customs Conference and on the Commission on Extraterritoriality, where it will be our policy so far as possible to meet the aspirations of China in all ways consistent with the interests of the countries involved.

COURT OF INTERNATIONAL JUSTICE

Pending before the Senate for nearly three years is the proposal to adhere to the protocol establishing the Permanent Court of International Justice. A well-established line of precedents mark America's effort to effect the establishment of a court of this nature. We took a leading part in laying the foundation on which it rests in the establishment of The Hague Court of Arbitration. It is that tribunal which nominates the judges who are elected by the Council and Assembly of the League of Nations.

The proposal submitted to the Senate was made dependent upon four conditions, the first of which is that by supporting the court we do not assume any obligations under the league; second, that we may participate upon an equality with other States in the election of judges; third, that the Congress shall determine what part of the expenses we shall bear; fourth, that the statute creating the court shall not be amended without our consent; and to these I have proposed an additional condition to the effect that we are not to be bound by advisory opinions rendered without our consent.

The court appears to be independent of the League. It is true the judges are elected by the Assembly and Council, but they are nominated by the Court of Arbitration, which we assisted to create and of which we are a part. The court was created by a statute, so-called, which is really a treaty made among some forty-eight different countries, that might properly be called a constitution of the court. This statute provides a method by which the judges are chosen, so that when the court of Arbitration nominates them and the Assembly and Council of the League elect them, they are not acting as instruments of the Court of Arbitration or instruments of the league, but as instruments of the statute.

This will be even more apparent if our representatives sit with the members of the council and assembly in electing the judges. . . .

The most careful provisions are made in the statute as to the qualifications of judges. . . .

We are not proposing to subject ourselves to any compulsory jurisdiction. If we support the court, we can never be obliged to submit any case which involves our interests for its decision. Our appearance before it would always be voluntary, for the purpose of presenting a case which we had agreed might be presented. There is no more danger that others might bring cases before the court involving our interests which we did not wish to have brought, after we have adhered, and probably not so much, than there would be of bringing such cases if we do not adhere. I think that we would have the same legal or moral right to disregard such a finding in the one case that we would in the other.

If we are going to support any court, it will not be one that we have set up alone or which reflects only our ideals. Other nations have their customs and their institutions, their thoughts and their methods of life. If a court is going to be international, its composition will have to yield to what is good in all these various elements. . . .

it is difficult to imagine anything that would be more helpful to the world than stability, tranquillity and international justice. . . .

FOREIGN DEBTS

Gradually, settlements have been made which provide for the liquidation of debts due to our Government from foreign governments. Those made with Great Britain, Finland, Hungary, Lithuania, and Poland have already been approved by the Congress. Since the adjournment, further agreements have been entered into with Belgium, Czechoslovakia, Latvia, Estonia, Italy, and Rumania. These 11 nations, which have already made settlements, represent $6,419,528,641 of the original principal of the loans. The principal sums without interest, still pending, are the debt of France, of $3,340,000,000; Greece,

$15,000,000; Yugoslavia, $51,000,000; Liberia, $26,000; Russia, $192,-
000,000, which those at present in control have undertaken openly
to repudiate; Nicaragua, $84,000, which is being paid currently; and
Austria, $24,000,000, on which by act of Congress a moratorium of
20 years has been granted. The only remaining sum is $12,000,000,
due from Armenia, which has now ceased to exist as an independent
nation.

In accordance with the settlements made, the amount of principal
and interest which is to be paid to the United States under these
agreements aggregates $15,200,688,253.93. It is obvious that the re-
maining settlements, which will undoubtedly be made, will bring this
sum up to an amount which will more than equal the principal due on
our present national debt. While these settlements are very large in
the aggregate, it has been felt that the terms granted were in all cases
very generous. . . .

ALIEN PROPERTY

Negotiations are progressing among the interested parties in relation to the final distribution of the assets in the hands of the Alien
Property Custodian. Our Government and people are interested as
creditors; the German Government and people are interested as debtors
and owners of the seized property. Pending the outcome of these negotiations, I do not recommend any affirmative legislation. For the
present we should continue in possession of this property which we hold
as security for the settlement of claims due to our people and our
Government.

IMMIGRATION

While not enough time has elapsed to afford a conclusive demon-
stration, such results as have been secured indicate that our immigration law is on the whole beneficial. It is undoubtedly a protection to the
wage earners of this country. The situation should, however, be carefully surveyed, in order to ascertain whether it is working a needless
hardship upon our own inhabitants. If it deprives them of the comfort
and society of those bound to them by close family ties, such modifications should be adopted as will afford relief. . . .

NATIONAL DEFENSE

Never before in time of peace has our country maintained so large
and effective a military force as it now has. The Army, Navy, Marine
Corps, National Guard, and Organized Reserves represent a strength
of about 558,400 men. These forces are well trained, well equipped,
and high in morale.

A sound selective service act giving broad authority for the mobilization in time of peril of all the resources of the country, both persons and materials, is needed to perfect our defensive policy in accordance with our ideals of equality. . . .

The Navy has the full treaty tonnage of capital ships. . . .

Last year at my suggestion the General Board of the Navy made an investigation and report on the relation of aircraft to warships. As a result authorizations and appropriations were made for more scout cruisers and fleet submarines and for completing aircraft carriers and equipping them with necessary planes. Additional training in aviation was begun at the Military and Naval Academies. A method of coordination and cooperation of the Army and Navy and the principal aircraft builders is being perfected. At the suggestion of the Secretaries of War and Navy I appointed a special board to make a further study of the problem of aircraft.

The report of the Air Board ought to be reassuring to the country, gratifying to the service and satisfactory to the Congress. It is thoroughly complete and represents the mature thought of the best talent in the country. No radical change in organization of the service seems necessary. . . .

Aviation is of great importance both for national defense and commercial development. We ought to proceed in its improvement by the necessary experiment and investigation. Our country is not behind in this art. . . .

VETERANS

If any one desires to estimate the esteem in which the veterans of America are held by their fellow citizens, it is but necessary to remember that the current budget calls for an expenditure of about $650,000,000 in their behalf. This is nearly the amount of the total cost of the National Government, exclusive of the Post Office, before we entered the last war.

At the two previous sessions of Congress legislation affecting veterans' relief was enacted and the law liberalized. This legislation brought into being a number of new provisions tending more nearly to meet the needs of our veterans, as well as afford the necessary authority to perfect the administration of these laws.

Experience with the new legislation so far has clearly demonstrated its constructive nature. It has increased the benefits received by many and has made eligible for benefits many others. Direct disbursements to the veteran or his dependents exceeding $21,000,000 have resulted, which otherwise would not have been made. The degree of utilization of our hospitals has increased through making facilities available to the incapacitated veteran regardless of service origin of the disability. This new legislation also has brought about a marked improvement of service to the veteran.

The organizations of ex-service men have proposed additional legislative changes which you will consider, but until the new law and the modifications made at the last session of Congress are given a more thorough test further changes in the basic law should be few and made only after careful though sympathetic consideration. . . .

AGRICULTURE

No doubt the position of agriculture as a whole has very much improved since the depression of three and four years ago. But there are many localities and many groups of individuals, apparently through no fault of their own, sometimes due to climatic conditions and sometimes to the prevailing price of a certain crop, still in a distressing condition. This is probably temporary, but it is none the less acute. National Government agencies, the Departments of Agriculture and Commerce, the Farm Loan Board, the intermediate credit banks, and the Federal Reserve Board are all cooperating to be of assistance and relief. On the other hand, there are localities and individuals who have had one of their most prosperous years. The general price level is fair, but here again there are exceptions both ways, some items being poor while others are excellent. In spite of a lessened production the farm income for this year will be about the same as last year and much above the three preceding years.

Agriculture is a very complex industry. It does not consist of one problem, but of several. They can not be solved at one stroke. They have to be met in different ways, and small gains are not to be despised.

It has appeared from all the investigations that I have been able to make that the farmers as a whole are determined to maintain the independence of their business. They do not wish to have meddling on the part of the Government or to be placed under the inevitable restrictions involved in any system of direct or indirect price-fixing, which would result from permitting the Government to operate in the agricultural markets. They are showing a very commendable skill in organizing themselves to transact their own business through cooperative marketing, which will this year turn over about $2,500,000,000, or nearly one-fifth of the total agricultural business. In this they are receiving help from the Government. The Department of Agriculture should be strengthened in this facility, in order to be able to respond when these marketing associations want help. While it ought not to undertake undue regulation, it should be equipped to give prompt information on crop prospects, supply, demand, current receipts, imports, exports, and prices.

A bill embodying these principles, which has been drafted under the advice and with the approval of substantially all the leaders and managers in the cooperative movement, will be presented to the Congress for its enactment. Legislation should also be considered to provide for leasing the unappropriated public domain for grazing purposes and adopting a uniform policy relative to grazing on the public lands and in the national forests. . . .

MUSCLE SHOALS

The problem of Muscle Shoals seems to me to have assumed a place all out of proportion with its real importance. It probably does not represent in market value much more than a first-class battleship, yet it has been discussed in the Congress over a period of years and for months at a time. It ought to be developed for the production of nitrates primarily, and incidentally for power purposes. This would serve defensive, agricultural, and industrial purposes. I am in favor of disposing of this property to meet these purposes. The findings of the special commission will be transmitted to the Congress for their information. I am convinced that the best possible disposition can be made by direct authorization of the Congress. As a means of negotiation I recommend the immediate appointment of a small joint special committee chosen from the appropriate general standing committees of the House and Senate to receive bids, which when made should be reported with recommendations as to acceptance, upon which a law should be enacted, effecting a sale to the highest bidder who will agree to carry out these purposes.

If anything were needed to demonstrate the almost utter incapacity of the National Government to deal directly with an industrial and commercial problem, it has been provided by our experience with this property. We have expended vast fortunes, we have taxed everybody, but we are unable to secure results which benefit anybody. This property ought to be transferred to private management under conditions which will dedicate it to the public purpose for which it was conceived.

RECLAMATION

The National Government is committed to a policy of reclamation and irrigation which it desires to establish on a sound basis and continue in the interest of the localities concerned. Exhaustive studies have recently been made of Federal reclamation, which have resulted in improving the projects and adjusting many difficulties. About one third of the projects is in good financial condition, another third can probably be made profitable, while the other third is under unfavorable conditions. The Congress has already provided for a survey which will soon be embodied in a report. That ought to suggest a method of relief which will make unnecessary further appeals to the Congress. Unless this can be done, Federal reclamation will be considerably retarded. . . .

SHIPPING

The maintenance of a merchant marine is of the utmost importance for national defense and the service of our commerce. We have a large number of ships engaged in that service. We also have a surplus supply, costly to care for, which ought to be sold. All the investigations that have been made under my direction, and those which have been prosecuted independently, have reached the conclusion that the fleet should be under the direct control of a single executive head, while the Shipping Board should exercise its judicial and regulatory functions in accordance with its original conceptions. . . . A plain and unmistakable reassertion of this principle of unified control, which I have always been advised was the intention of the Congress to apply, is necessary to increase the efficiency of our merchant fleet.

COAL

The perennial conflict in the coal industry is still going on to the great detriment of the wage earners, the owners, and especially to the public. With deposits of coal in this country capable of supplying its needs for hundreds of years, inability to manage and control this great resource for the benefit of all concerned is very close to a national economic failure. It has been the subject of repeated investigation and reiterated recommendation. Yet the industry seems never to have accepted modern methods of adjusting differences between employers and employees. The industry could serve the public much better and become subject to a much more effective method of control if regional consolidations and more freedom in the formation of marketing associations, under the supervision of the Department of Commerce, were permitted.

At the present time the National Government has little or no authority to deal with this vital necessity of the life of the country. It has permitted itself to remain so powerless that its only attitude must be humble supplication. Authority should be lodged with the President and the Departments of Commerce and Labor, giving them power to deal with an emergency. . . .

PROHIBITION

Under the orderly processes of our fundamental institutions the Constitution was lately amended providing for national prohibition.

The Congress passed an act for its enforcement, and similar acts have been provided by most of the States. It is the law of the land. It is the duty of all who come under its jurisdiction to observe the spirit of that law, and it is the duty of the Department of Justice and the Treasury Department to enforce it. . . .

WATERWAY DEVELOPMENT

For many years our country has been employed in plans and operations for the development of our intracoastal and inland waterways. This work along our coast is an important adjunct to our commerce. It will be carried on, together with the further opening up of our harbors, as our resources permit. The Government made an agreement during the war to take over the Cape Cod Canal, under which the owners made valuable concessions. This pledged faith of the Government ought to be redeemed.

Two other main fields are under consideration. One is the Great Lakes and St. Lawrence, including the Erie Canal. This includes stabilizing the lake level, and is both a waterway and power project. A joint commission of the United States and Canada is working on plans and surveys which will not be completed until next April. . . . The other is the Mississippi River system. This is almost entirely devoted to navigation. Work on the Ohio River will be completed in about three years. A modern channel connecting Chicago, New Orleans, Kansas City, and Pittsburgh should be laid out and work on the tributaries prosecuted. Some work is being done of a preparatory nature along the Missouri, and large expenditures are being made yearly in the lower reaches of the Mississippi and its tributaries which contribute both to flood control and navigation. Preliminary measures are being taken on the Colorado River project, which is exceedingly important for flood control, irrigation, power development, and water supply to the area concerned. . . .

The Government has already expended large sums upon scientific research and engineering investigation in promotion of this Colorado River project. The actual progress has been retarded for many years by differences among the seven States in the basin over their relative water rights and among different groups as to methods. In an attempt to settle the primary difficulty of the water rights, Congress authorized the Colorado River Commission which agreed on November 24, 1922, upon an interstate compact to settle these rights, subject to the ratification of the State legislatures and Congress. All seven States except Arizona at one time ratified, the Arizona Legislature making certain reservations which failed to meet the approval of the governor. Subsequently an attempt was made to establish the compact upon a six-State basis, but in this case California imposed reservations. There appears to be no division of opinion upon the major principles of the compact, but difficulty in separating contentions as to methods of development from the discussion of it. . . . Because of all this difference of view it is most desirable that Congress should consider the creation of some agency that will be able to determine methods of improvement solely upon economic and engineering facts, that would be authorized to negotiate and settle, subject to the approval of Congress, the participation, rights, and obligations of each group in any particular works. . . .

WATER POWER

Along with the development of navigation should go every possible encouragement for the development of our water power. While steam still plays a dominant part, this is more and more becoming an era of electricity. Once installed, the cost is moderate, has not tended greatly to increase, and is entirely free from the unavoidable dirt and disagreeable features attendant upon the burning of coal. Every facility should be extended for the connection of the various units into a superpower plant, capable at all times of a current increasing uniformity over the entire system.

RAILROADS

The railroads throughout the country are in a fair state of prosperity. Their service is good and their supply of cars is abundant. Their condition would be improved and the public better served by a system of consolidations. . . .

It is gratifying to report that both the railroad managers and railroad employees are providing boards for the mutual adjustment of differences in harmony with the principles of conference, conciliation, and arbitration. . . .

A strike in modern industry has many of the aspects of war in the modern world. It injures labor and it injures capital. If the industry involved is a basic one, it reduces the necessary economic surplus and, increasing the cost of living, it injures the economic welfare and general comfort of the whole people. It also involves a deeper cost. It tends to embitter and divide the community into warring classes and thus weakens the unity and power of our national life. . . .

OUTLYING POSSESSIONS

The time has come for careful investigation of the expenditures and success of the laws by which we have undertaken to administer our outlying possessions. . . .

MOTHERS' AID

The Government ought always to be alert on the side of the humanities. It ought to encourage provisions for economic justice for the defenseless. It ought to extend its relief through its national and local agencies, as may be appropriate in each case, to the suffering and the needy. It ought to be charitable.

Although more than 40 of our States have enacted measures in aid of motherhood, the District of Columbia is still without such a law. A carefully considered bill will be presented, which ought to have most thoughtful consideration in order that the Congress may adopt a measure which will be hereafter a model for all parts of the Union.

CIVIL SERVICE

In 1883 the Congress passed the civil service act, which from a modest beginning of 14,000 employees has grown until there are now 425,000 in the classified service. This has removed the clerical force of the Nation from the wasteful effects of the spoils system and made it more stable and efficient. The time has come to consider classifying all postmasters, collectors of customs, collectors of internal revenue, and prohibition agents, by an act covering those at present in office, except when otherwise provided by Executive order.

The necessary statistics are now being gathered to form the basis of a valuation of the civil service retirement fund based on current conditions of the service. . . .

REORGANIZATION

No final action has yet been taken on the measure providing for the reorganization of the various departments. I therefore suggest that this measure, which will be of great benefit to the efficient and economical administration of the business of the Government, be brought forward and passed.

THE NEGRO

Nearly one-tenth of our population consists of the Negro race. The progress which they have made in all the arts of civilization in the last 60 years is almost beyond belief. Our country has no more loyal citizens. But they do still need sympathy, kindness, and helpfulness. . . .

CONCLUSION

It is apparent that we are reaching into an era of great general prosperity. It will continue only so long as we shall use it properly.

After all, there is but a fixed quantity of wealth in this country at any fixed time. The only way that we can all secure more of it is to create more. The element of time enters into production. If the people have sufficient moderation and contentment to be willing to improve their condition by the process of enlarging production, eliminating waste, and distributing equitably, a prosperity almost without limit lies before us. If the people are to be dominated by selfishness, seeking immediate riches by nonproductive speculation and by wasteful quarreling over the returns from industry, they will be confronted by the inevitable results of depression and privation. If they will continue industrious and thrifty, contented with fair wages and moderate profits, and the returns which accrue from the development of our natural resources, our prosperity will extend itself indefinitely.

In all your deliberations you should remember that the purpose of legislation is to translate principles into action. It is an effort to have our country be better by doing better. Because the thought and ways of people are firmly fixed and not easily changed, the field within which immediate improvement can be secured is very narrow. Legislation can provide opportunity. Whether it is taken advantage of or not depends upon the people themselves. The Government of the United States has been created by the people. It is solely responsible to them. It will be most successful if it is conducted solely for their benefit. All its efforts would be of little avail unless they brought more justice, more enlightenment, more happiness and prosperity into the home. This means an opportunity to observe religion, secure education, and earn a living under a reign of law and order. It is the growth and improvement of the material and spiritual life of the Nation. We shall not be able to gain these ends merely by our own action. If they come at all, it will be because we have been willing to work in harmony with the abiding purpose of a Divine Providence.

CALVIN COOLIDGE

MESSAGE ON NICARAGUA
January 10, 1927

*In a message to both houses of Congress, President
Coolidge reviewed the history of disturbances in Nicaragua and the reasons he had sent marines there the month
before at the request of General Diaz, whom the United
States had recognized as president. Juan Sacasa was
leader of the rebels opposing Diaz. The dissension followed withdrawal of American troops in 1925. Coolidge
sent Henry L. Stimson to Nicaragua in April, 1927, to try
to settle the problem. Marines remained in the Central
American nation until 1933.*

To the Congress of the United States:

. . . in 1912 the United States intervened in Nicaragua with a large
force and put down a revolution, and . . . from that time to 1925 a
legation guard of American marines was, with the consent of the
Nicaraguan Government, kept in Managua to protect American lives
and property. In 1923 representatives of the five Central American
countries, namely, Costa Rica, Guatemala, Honduras, Nicaragua, and
Salvador, at the invitation of the United States, met in Washington and
entered into a series of treaties. These treaties dealt with limitation
of armament, a Central American tribunal for arbitration, and the general subject of peace and amity. The treaty last referred to specifically provides in Article II that the Governments of the contracting parties
will not recognize any other government which may come into power in
any of the five Republics through a coup d'etat, or revolution. . . .

Immediately following the inauguration of President Diaz and frequently since that date he has appealed to the United States for support,
has informed this Government of the aid which Mexico is giving to the
revolutionists, and has stated that he is unable solely because of the aid
given by Mexico to the revolutionists to protect the lives and property
of American citizens and other foreigners. . . .

Doctor Sacasa . . . placed himself at the head of the insurrection
and declared himself President of Nicaragua. He has never been recognized by any of the Central American Republics nor by any other
government, with the exception of Mexico, which recognized him immediately. As arms and munitions in large quantities were reaching
the revolutionists, I deemed it unfair to prevent the recognized government from purchasing arms abroad, and, accordingly, the Secretary of
State has notified the Diaz Government that licenses would be issued
for the export of arms and munitions purchased in this country. . . .

There is no question that if the revolution continues American investments and business interests in Nicaragua will be very seriously
affected, if not destroyed.

Manifestly the relation of this Government to the Nicaraguan situation and its policy in the existing emergency, are determined by the facts which I have described. The proprietary rights of the United States in the Nicaraguan canal route, with the necessary implications growing out of it affecting the Panama Canal, together with the obligations flowing from the investments of all classes of our citizens in Nicaragua, place us in a position of peculiar responsibility. I am sure it is not the desire of the United States to intervene in the internal affairs of Nicaragua or of any other Central American Republic. Nevertheless it must be said that we have a very definite and special interest in the maintenance of order and good government in Nicaragua at the present time, and that the stability, prosperity, and independence of all Central American countries can never be a matter of indifference to us. The United States can not, therefore, fail to view with deep concern any serious threat to stability and constitutional government in Nicaragua tending toward anarchy and jeopardizing American interests, especially if such state of affairs is contributed to or brought about by outside influences or by any foreign power. It has always been and remains the policy of the United States in such circumstances to take the steps that may be necessary for the preservation and protection of the lives, the property, and the interests of its citizens and of this Government itself. In this respect I propose to follow the path of my predecessors. . . .

FOURTH ANNUAL MESSAGE
December 7, 1926

In a message which repeated substantially his prior mes-
sages to Congress, Coolidge also called for legislation
to enable him to deal with possible emergencies in the
coal industry, and asked for prompt enactment of branch-
banking laws.

Members of the Congress:

In reporting to the Congress the state of the Union, I find it impossible to characterize it other than one of general peace and prosperity.
In some quarters our diplomacy is vexed with difficult and as yet un-
solved problems, but nowhere are we met with armed conflict. If
some occupations and areas are not flourishing, in none does there
remain any acute chronic depressions. . . .

ECONOMY

Our present state of prosperity has been greatly promoted by
three important causes, one of which is economy, resulting in reduction and reform in national taxation. Another is the elimination of many
kinds of waste. The third is a general raising of the standards of efficiency. . . .

I am convinced that it would be greatly for the welfare of the country if we avoid at the present session all commitments except those
of the most pressing nature. From a reduction of the debt and taxes
will accrue a wider benefit to all the people of this country than from
embarking on any new enterprise. When our war debt is decreased we
shall have resources for expansion. Until that is accomplished we
should confine ourselves to expenditures of the most urgent necessity.

The Department of Commerce has performed a most important
function in making plans and securing support of all kinds of national
enterprise for the elimination of waste. Efficiency has been greatly
promoted through good management and the constantly increasing cooperation of the wage earners throughout the whole realm of private
business. It is my opinion that this whole development has been pred-
icated on the foundation of a protective tariff.

TAX REDUCTION

As a result of economy of administration by the Executive and of
appropriation by the Congress, the end of this fiscal year will leave a

surplus in the Treasury estimated at $383,000,000. Unless otherwise ordered, such surplus is used for the retirement of the war debt. . . . Whenever the state of the Treasury will permit, I believe in a reduction of taxation. I think the taxpayers are entitled to it. But I am not advocating tax reduction merely for the benefit of the taxpayer; I am advocating it for the benefit of the country.

If it appeared feasible, I should welcome permanent tax reduction at this time. . . . Meantime, it is possible to grant some real relief by a simple measure making reductions in the payments which accrue on the 15th of March and June, 1927. . . .

PROTECTIVE TARIFF

It is estimated that customs receipts for the present fiscal year will exceed $615,000,000, the largest which were ever secured from that source. The value of our imports for the last fiscal year was $4,466,-000,000, an increase of more than 71 per cent since the present tariff law went into effect. Of these imports about 65 per cent, or, roughly, $2,900,000,000, came in free of duty, which means that the United States affords a duty-free market to other countries almost equal in value to the total imports of Germany and greatly exceeding the total imports of France. We have admitted a greater volume of free imports than any other country except England. . . .

Those who are starting an agitation for a reduction of tariff duties partly at least for the benefit of those to whom money has been lent abroad, ought to know that there does not seem to be a very large field within the area of our imports in which probable reductions would be advantageous to foreign goods. Those who wish to benefit foreign producers are much more likely to secure that result by continuing the present enormous purchasing power which comes from our prosperity that has increased our imports over 71 per cent in four years than from any advantages that are likely to accrue from a general tariff reduction.

AGRICULTURE

. . . While some localities and some particular crops furnish exceptions, in general agriculture is continuing to make progress in recovering from the depression of 1921 and 1922. Animal products and food products are in a more encouraging position, while cotton, due to the high prices of past years supplemented by ideal weather conditions, has been stimulated to a point of temporary overproduction. Acting on the request of the cotton-growing interests, I appointed a committee to assist in carrying out their plans. As a result of this cooperation sufficient funds have been pledged to finance the storage and carrying of 4,000,000 bales of cotton. . . .

There is agreement on all sides that some portions of our agricultural industry have lagged behind other industries in recovery from the war and that further improvement in methods of marketing of agricultural products is most desirable. There is belief also that the Federal Government can further contribute to these ends beyond the many helpful measures taken during the last five years through the different acts of Congress for advancing the interests of the farmers.

The packers and stockyards act,

Establishing of the Intermediate credit banks for agricultural purposes,

The Purnell Act for agricultural research,

The Capper-Volstead Cooperative Marketing Act,

The cooperative marketing act of 1926,

Amendments to the warehousing act,

The enlargement of the activities of the Department of Agriculture,

Enlargement of the scope of loans by the Farm Loan Board,

The tariff on agricultural products,

The large Federal expenditure in improvement of waterways and highways,

The reduction of Federal taxes,

in all comprise a great series of government actions in the advancement of the special interest of agriculture.

In determination of what further measures may be undertaken it seems to me there are certain pitfalls which must be avoided and our test in avoiding them should be to avoid disaster to the farmer himself.

Acting upon my recommendation, the Congress has ordered the Interstate Commerce Commission to investigate the freight-rate structure, directing that such changes shall be made in freight rates as will promote freedom of movement of agricultural products. Railroad consolidation which I am advocating would also result in a situation where rates could be made more advantageous for farm produce, as has recently been done in the revision of rates on fertilizers in the South. Additional benefit will accrue from the development of our inland waterways. . . .

The advantages to be derived from a more comprehensive and less expensive system of transportation for agriculture ought to be supplemented by provision for an adequate supply of fertilizer at a lower cost than it is at present obtainable. This advantage we are attempting to secure by the proposed development at Muscle Shoals, and there are promising experiments being made in synthetic chemistry for the production of nitrates.

A survey should be made of the relation of Government grazing lands to the livestock industry. Additional legislation is desirable more definitely to establish the place of grazing in the administration of the national forests, properly subordinated to their functions of producing timber and conserving the water supply. . . .

Attention is again directed to the surplus problem of agriculture by the present cotton situation. Surpluses often affect prices of various farm commodities in a disastrous manner, and the problem urgently demands a solution. Discussions both in and out of Congress during the past few years have given us a better understanding of the subject, and it is my hope that out of the various proposals made the basis will be found for a sound and effective solution upon which agreement can be reached. In my opinion cooperative marketing associations will be important aids to the ultimate solution of the problem. It may well be, however, that additional measures will be needed to supplement their efforts. . . .

The whole question of agriculture needs most careful consideration. In the past few years the Government has given this subject more attention than any other subject. While the Government is not to be blamed for failure to perform the impossible, the agricultural regions are entitled to know that they have its constant solicitude and sympathy. Many of the farmers are burdened with debts and taxes which they are unable to carry. We are expending in this country many millions of dollars each year to increase farm production. We ought now to put more emphasis on the question of farm marketing. If a sound solution of a permanent nature can be found for this problem, the Congress ought not to hesitate to adopt it.

In previous messages I have referred to the national importance of the proper development of our water resources. The great projects of extension of the Mississippi system, the protection and development of the lower Colorado River, are before Congress, and I have previously commented upon them. I favor the necessary legislation to expedite these projects. . . .

RECLAMATION

It is increasingly evident that the Federal Government must in the future take a leading part in the impounding of water for conservation with incidental power for the development of the irrigable lands of the arid region. The unused waters of the West are found mainly in large rivers. Works to store and distribute these have such magnitude and cost that they are not attractive to private enterprise. . . .

MERCHANT MARINE

It is axiomatic that no agricultural and industrial country can get the full benefit of its own advantages without a merchant marine. We have been proceeding under the act of Congress that contemplates the establishment of trade routes to be ultimately transferred to private ownership and operation. Due to temporary conditions abroad and at home we have a large demand just now for certain types of freight vessels. Some suggestion has been made for new construction. I do not feel that we are yet warranted in entering that field. Such ships as we might build could not be sold after they are launched for anywhere near what they would cost. . . .

RADIO LEGISLATION

The Department of Commerce has for some years urgently presented the necessity for further legislation in order to protect radio listeners from interference between broadcasting stations and to carry out other regulatory functions. Both branches of Congress at the last session passed enactments intended to effect such regulation, but the two bills yet remain to be brought into agreement and final passage.

Due to decisions of the courts, the authority of the department under the law of 1912 has broken down; many more stations have been operating than can be accommodated within limited number of wave lengths available; further stations are in course of construction; many stations have departed from the scheme of allocation set down by the department, and the whole service of this most important public function has drifted into such chaos as seems likely, if not remedied, to destroy its great value. I most urgently recommend that this legislation should be speedily enacted. . . .

BITUMINOUS COAL

No progress appears to have been made within large areas of the bituminous coal industry toward creation of voluntary machinery by which greater assurance can be given to the public of peaceful adjustment of wage difficulties such as has been accomplished in the anthracite industry. This bituminous industry is one of primary necessity and bears a great responsibility to the Nation for continuity of supplies. As the wage agreements in the unionized section of the industry expire on April 1 next, and as conflicts may result which may imperil public interest, and have for many years often called for action of the Executive in protection of the public, I again recommend the passage of such legislation as will assist the Executive in dealing with such emergencies through a special temporary board of conciliation and mediation and through administrative agencies for the purpose of distribution of coal and protection of the consumers of coal from profiteering. At present the Executive is not only without authority to act but is actually prohibited by law from making any expenditure to meet the emergency of a coal famine.

JUDICIARY

The Federal courts hold a high position in the administration of justice in the world. While individual judicial officers have sometimes been subjected to just criticism, the courts as a whole have maintained an exceedingly high standard. The Congress may well consider the question of supplying fair salaries and conferring upon the Supreme Court the same rule-making power on the law side of the district courts that they have always possessed on the equity side. A bill is also pending providing for retirement after a certain number of years of service, although they have not been consecutive, which should have your favorable consideration. These faithful servants of the Government are about the last that remain to be provided for in the postwar readjustments.

BANKING

There has been pending in Congress for nearly three years banking legislation to clarify the national bank act and reasonably to increase the powers of the national banks. I believe that within the limitation of sound banking principles Congress should now and for the future place the national banks upon a fair equality with their competitors, the State banks, and I trust that means may be found so that the differences on branch-banking legislation between the Senate and the House of Representatives may be settled along sound lines and the legislation promptly enacted.

It would be difficult to overestimate the service which the Federal reserve system has already rendered to the country. It is necessary only to recall the chaotic condition of our banking organization at the time the Federal reserve system was put into operation. The old system consisted of a vast number of independent banking units, with scattered bank reserves which never could be mobilized in times of greatest need. In spite of vast banking resources, there was no coordination of reserves or any credit elasticity. As a consequence, a strain was felt even during crop-moving periods and when it was necessary to meet other seasonal and regularly recurring needs.

The Federal reserve system is not a panacea for all economic or financial ills. It can not prevent depression in certain industries which are experiencing overexpansion of production or contraction of their markets. Its business is to furnish adequate credit and currency facilities. This it has succeeded in doing, both during the war and in the more difficult period of deflation and readjustment which followed. It enables us to look to the future with confidence and to make plans far ahead, based on the belief that the Federal reserve system will exercise a steadying influence on credit conditions and thereby prevent any sudden or severe reactions from the period of prosperity which we are now enjoying. In order that these plans may go forward, action should be taken at the present session on the question of renewing the banks' charters and thereby insuring a continuation of the policies and present usefulness of the Federal reserve system.

FEDERAL REGULATION

I am in favor of reducing, rather than expanding, Government bureaus which seek to regulate and control the business activities of the people. . . . It is too much assumed that because an abuse exists it is the business of the National Government to provide a remedy. The presumption should be that it is the business of local and State governments. Such national action results in encroaching upon the salutary independence of the States and by undertaking to supersede their natural authority fills the land with bureaus and departments which are undertaking to do what it is impossible for them to accomplish and brings our whole system of government into disrespect and disfavor. . . .

INSULAR POSSESSIONS

This Government holds in sacred trusteeship islands which it has acquired in the East and West Indies. In all of them the people are more prosperous than at any previous time. A system of good roads, education, and general development is in progress. The people are better governed than ever before and generally content.

In the Philippine Islands Maj. Gen. Leonard Wood has been Governor General for five years and has administered his office with tact and ability greatly to the success of the Filipino people. These are a proud and sensitive race, who are making such progress with our cooperation that we can view the results of this experiment with great satisfaction. As we are attempting to assist this race toward self-government, we should look upon their wishes with great respect, granting their requests immediately when they are right, yet maintaining a frank firmness in refusing when they are wrong. We shall measure their progress in no small part by their acceptance of the terms of the organic law under which the islands are governed and their faithful observance of its provisions. . . .

In order that these possessions might suffer no seeming neglect, I have recently sent Col. Carmi A. Thompson to the islands to make a survey in cooperation with the Governor General to suggest what might be done to improve conditions. Later, I may make a more extended report including recommendations. The economic development of the islands is very important. They ought not to be turned back to the people until they are both politically fitted for self-government and economically independent. . . .

NATIONAL DEFENSE

Our policy of national defense is not one of making war, but of insuring peace. The land and sea force of America, both in its domestic and foreign implications, is distinctly a peace force. It is an arm of the police power to guarantee order and the execution of the law at home and security to our citizens abroad. . . .

. . . For years we have besought nations to disarm. We have recently expressed our willingness at Geneva to enter into treaties for the limitation of all types of warships according to the ratio adopted at the Washington Conference. This offer is still pending. While we are and shall continue to be armed it is not as a menace, but rather a common assurance of tranquillity to all the peace-loving people of the world. For us to do any less would be to disregard our obligations, evade our responsibilities, and jeopardize our national honor.

VETERANS

. . . The main unfinished feature is that of hospitalization. This requirement is being rapidly met. Various veteran bodies will present to you recommendations which should have your careful consideration. At the last session we increased our annual expenditure for pensions and relief on account of the veterans of three wars. While I approve of proper relief for all suffering, I do not favor any further extension of our pension system at this time. . . .

PROHIBITION

The duly authorized public authorities of this country have made prohibition the law of the land. . . . Officers of the Department of Justice throughout the country should be vigilant in enforcing the law, but local authorities, which had always been mainly responsible for the enforcement of law in relation to intoxicating liquor, ought not to seek evasion by attempting to shift the burden wholly upon the Federal agencies. . . .

FOREIGN RELATIONS

. . . It is because of our historical detachment and the generations of comparative indifference toward us by other nations that our public is inclined to consider altogether too seriously the reports that we are criticized abroad. We never had a larger foreign trade than at the the present time. Our good offices were never more sought and the necessity for our assistance and cooperation was never more universally declared in any time of peace. . . .

A special conference on the Chinese customs tariff provided for by the treaty between the nine powers relating to the Chinese customs tariff signed at Washington on February 6, 1922, was called by the Chinese Government to meet at Peking on October 26, 1925. We participated in this conference through fully empowered delegates and, with good will, endeavored to cooperate with the other participating powers with a view to putting into effect promises made to China at the Washington conference, and considering any reasonable proposal that might be made by the Chinese Government for the revision of the treaties on the subject of China's tariff. With these aims in view the American delegation at the outset of the conference proposed to put into effect the surtaxes provided for by the Washington treaty and to proceed immediately to the negotiation of a treaty, which, among other things, was to make provision for the abolition of taxes collected on goods in transit, remove the tariff restrictions in existing treaties, and put into effect the national tariff law of China.

Early in April of the present year the central Chinese Government was ousted from power by opposing warring factions. It became impossible under the circumstances to continue the negotiations. Finally, on July 3, the delegates of the foreign powers, including those of the United States, issued a statement expressing their unanimous and earnest desire to proceed with the work of the conference at the earliest possible moment when the delegates of the Chinese Government are in a position to resume discussions with the foreign delegates of the problems before the conference. We are prepared to resume the negotiations thus interrupted whenever a Government representing the Chinese people and acting on their behalf presents itself. The fact that constant warfare between contending Chinese factions has rendered it impossible to bring these negotiations to a successful conclusion is a matter of deep regret. Throughout these conflicts we have maintained a position of the most careful neutrality. Our naval vessels in Asiatic waters, pursuant to treaty rights, have been used only for the protection of American citizens.

Silas H. Strawn, Esq., was sent to China as American commissioner to cooperate with commissioners of the other powers in the establishment of a commission to inquire into the present practice of extraterritorial jurisdiction in China, with a view to reporting to the Governments of the several powers their findings of fact in regard to these matters. The commission commenced its work in January, 1926, and agreed upon a joint report which was signed on September 16, 1926. The commission's report has been received and is being studied with a view to determining our future policy in regard to the question of extraterritorial privileges under treaties between the United States and China.

The Preparatory Commission for the Disarmament Conference met at Geneva on May 18 and its work has been proceeding almost continuously since that date. It would be premature to attempt to form a judgment as to the progress that has been made. The commission had had before it a comprehensive list of questions touching upon all aspects of the question of the limitation of armament. In the commission's discussions many differences of opinion have developed. However, I am hopeful that at least some measure of agreement will be reached as the discussions continue. The American representation on the commission has consistently tried to be helpful, and has kept before it the practical objective to which the commission is working, namely, actual agreements for the limitation of armaments. Our representatives will continue their work in that direction.

One of the most encouraging features of the commission's work thus far has been the agreement in principle among the naval experts of a majority of the powers parties to the Washington treaty limiting naval armament upon methods and standards for the comparison and further limitation of naval armament. . . .

THE CAPITAL CITY

We are embarking on an ambitious building program for the city of Washington. The Memorial Bridge is under way with all that it holds for use and beauty. New buildings are soon contemplated. This program should represent the best that exists in the art and science of architecture. Into these structures which must be considered as of a permanent nature ought to go the aspirations of the Nation, its ideals expressed in forms of beauty. . . .

AMERICAN IDEALS

America is not and must not be a country without ideals. They are useless if they are only visionary; they are only valuable if they are practical. A nation can not dwell constantly on the mountain tops. It has to be replenished and sustained through the ceaseless toil of the less inspiring valleys. But its face ought always to be turned upward, its vision ought always to be fixed on high.

We need ideals that can be followed in daily life, that can be traslated into terms of the home. We can not expect to be relieved from toil, but we do expect to divest it of degrading conditions. Work is honorable; it is entitled to an honorable recompense. We must strive mightily, but having striven there is a defect in our political and social system if we are not in general rewarded with success. To relieve the land of the burdens that came from the war, to release to the individual more of the fruits of his own industry, to increase his earning capacity and decrease his hours of labor, to enlarge the circle of his vision through good roads and better transportation, to place before him the opportunity for education both in science and in art, to leave him free to receive the inspiration of religion, all these are ideals which deliver him from the servitude of the body and exalt him to the service of the soul. Through this emancipation from the things that are material, we broaden our dominion over the things that are spiritual.

McGRAIN v. DAUGHERTY
January 17, 1927

This Supreme Court decision established that Congress could compel the testimony of witnesses as part of its legislative function. The defendant, Mally S. Daugherty, was president of Midland National Bank of Washington Court House, Ohio, and brother of the former Attorney General. A warrant had been issued for him when he twice refused to appear at a Senate investigation of his brother and to bring bank records.

. . . We are of opinion that the power of inquiry — with process to enforce it — is an essential and appropriate auxiliary to the legislative function. It was so regarded and employed in American legislatures before the Constitution was framed and ratified. . . .

A legislative body cannot legislate wisely or effectively in the absence of information respecting the conditions which the legislation is intended to affect or change; and where the legislative body does not itself possess the requisite information — which not infrequently is true — recourse must be had to others who do possess it. Experience has taught that mere requests for such information often are unavailing, and also that information which is volunteered is not always accurate or complete; so some means of compulsion are essential to obtain what is needed. . . .

The contention is earnestly made on behalf of the witness that this power of inquiry, if sustained, may be abusively and oppressively exerted. If this be so, it affords no ground for denying the power. The same contention might be directed against the power to legislate, and of course would be unavailing. . . .

We are of the opinion that . . . it sufficiently appears, when the proceedings are rightly interpreted, that the object of the investigation and of the effort to secure the witness's testimony was to obtain information for legislative purposes.

It is quite true that the resolution directing the investigation does not in terms avow that it is intended to be in aid of legislation; but it does show that the subject to be investigated was the administration of the Department of Justice — whether its functions were being properly discharged or were being neglected or misdirected, and particularly whether the Attorney General and his assistants were performing or neglecting their duties in respect of the institution and prosecution of proceedings to punish crimes and enforce appropriate remedies against the wrongdoers — specific instances of alleged neglect being recited. Plainly the subject was one on which legislation could be had and would be materially aided by the information which the investigation was calculated to elicit. . . .

The second resolution — the one directing that the witness be attached — declares that his testimony is sought with the purpose of obtaining "information necessary as a basis for such legislative and other action as the Senate may deem necessary and proper." This avowal of contemplated legislation is in accord with what we think is the right interpretation of the earlier resolution directing the investigation. The suggested possibility of "other action" if deemed "necessary or proper" is of course open to criticism in that there is no other action in the matter which would be within the power of the Senate. But we do not assent to the view that this indefinite and untenable suggestion invalidates the entire proceeding. . . .

We conclude that the investigation was ordered for a legitimate object; that the witness wrongfully refused to appear and testify before the committee and was lawfully attached; that the Senate is entitled to have him give testimony pertinent to the inquiry, either at its bar or before the committee; and that the district court erred in discharging him from custody under the attachment. . . .

McNARY-HAUGEN BILL
February 25, 1927

Coolidge strongly opposed the McNary-Haugen plan to aid the American farmer by getting rid of surpluses abroad at a loss, if necessary, and reimbursing the farmer. The postwar economic plight of the farmer was a major and longlasting problem of Coolidge's time in office.

SEC. 1. It is hereby declared to be the policy of Congress to promote the orderly marketing of basic agricultural commodities in interstate and foreign commerce and to that end to provide for the control and disposition of surpluses of such commodities, to enable producers of such commodities to stabilize their markets against undue and excessive fluctuations, to preserve advantageous domestic markets for such commodities, to minimize speculation and waste in marketing such commodities, and to encourage the organization of producers of such commodities into cooperative marketing associations.

SEC. 2. (a) A Federal Farm Board is hereby created which shall consist of the Secretary of Agriculture, who shall be a member ex officio, and 12 members, one from each of the 12 Federal land-bank districts, appointed by the President of the United States, by and with the advice and consent of the Senate, from lists of eligibles submitted by the nominating committee for the district, as hereinafter in this section provided.

(b) There is hereby established a nominating committee in each of the 12 Federal land-bank districts, to consist of seven members. Four of the members of the nominating committee in each district shall be elected by the bona fide farm organizations and cooperative associations in such district at a convention of such organizations and associations,. . . Two of the members of the nominating committee in each district shall be elected by a majority vote of the heads of the agricultural departments of the several States of each Federal land-bank district, . . . One of the members of the nominating committee in each district shall be appointed by the Secretary of Agriculture. . . .

SEC. 6. (a) For the purposes of this act, cotton, wheat, corn, rice, tobacco, and swine shall be known and are referred to as "basic agricultural commodities,''. . .

(b) Whenever the board finds that the conditions of production and marketing of any other agricultural commodity are such that the provisions of this act applicable to a basic agricultural commodity should be made applicable to such other agricultural commodity, the board shall submit its report thereon to Congress.

(c) Whenever the board finds, first, that there is or may be during the ensuing year either (1) a surplus above the domestic requirements for wheat, corn, rice, tobacco, or swine, or (2) a surplus above the requirements for the orderly marketing of cotton, or of wheat, corn, rice, tobacco, or swine; and, second, that both the advisory council hereinafter created for the commodity and a substantial number of cooperative associations or other organizations representing the producers of the commodity favor the full cooperation of the board in the stabilization of the commodity, then the board shall publicly declare its findings and commence, upon a date to be fixed by the board and published in such declaration, the operations in such commodity authorized by this act: . . .

(d) During the continuance of such operations in any basic agricultural commodity, the board is authorized to enter into agreements, for the purpose of carrying out the policy declared in section 1, with any cooperative association engaged in handling the basic agricultural commodity, or with a corporation created by one or more of such cooperative associations, or with processors of the basic agricultural commodity.

(e) Such agreements may provide for (1) removing or disposing of any surplus of the basic agricultural commodity, (2) withholding such surplus, (3) insuring such commodity against undue and excessive fluctuations in market conditions, and (4) financing the purchase, storage, or sale or other disposition of the commodity. . . .

SEC. 8. In order that each marketed unit of a basic agricultural commodity may contribute ratably its equitable share to the stabilization fund hereinafter established for such commodity; in order to prevent any unjust discrimination against, any direct burden or undue restraint upon, and any suppression of commerce with foreign nations in basic agricultural commodities in favor of interstate or intrastate commerce in such commodities — there shall be apportioned and paid as a regulation of such commerce an equalization fee as hereinafter provided.

SEC. 9. Prior to the commencement of operations in respect of any basic agricultural commodity, and thereafter from time to time, the board shall estimate the probable advances, losses, costs, and charges to be paid in respect of the operations in such commodity. Having due regard to such estimates, the board shall from time to time determine and publish the amount for each unit of weight, measure, or value designated by it, to be collected upon such unit of such basic agricultural commodity during the operations in such commodity. Such amount is hereinafter referred to as the "equalization fee". . .

SEC. 10. (a) Under such regulations as the board may prescribe there shall be paid. . . an equalization fee upon one of the following: the transportation, processing, or sale of such unit. . . .

(b)   The board may by regulation require any person engaged in the transportation, processing, or acquisition by sale of a basic agricultural commodity —

(1)   To file returns under oath and to report, in respect of his transportation, processing, or acquisition of such commodity, the amount of equalization fees payable thereon and such other facts as may be necessary for their payment or collection.

(2)   To collect the equalization fee as directed by the board, and to account therefor.

(3)   In the case of cotton, to issue to the producer a serial receipt for the commodity which shall be evidence of the participating interest of the producer in the equalization fund for the commodity. . . .

SEC. 11.   (a)   In accordance with regulations prescribed by the board, there shall be established a stabilization fund for each basic agricultural commodity. Such funds shall be administered by and exclusively under the control of the board, and the board shall have the exclusive power of expending the moneys in any such fund. . . .

SEC. 12.   (a)   The board is authorized, upon such terms and conditions and in accordance with such regulations as it may prescribe, to make loans out of the revolving fund to any cooperative association engaged in the purchase, storage, or sale or other disposition of any agricultural commodity (whether or not a basic agricultural commodity) for the purpose of assisting such cooperative association in controlling the surplus of such commodity in excess of the requirements for orderly marketing.

(b)   For the purpose of developing continuity of cooperative services, including unified terminal marketing facilities and equipment, the board is authorized, upon such terms and conditions and in accordance with such regulations as it may prescribe, to make loans out of the revolving fund to any cooperative association engaged in the purchase, storage, sale, or other disposition, or processing of any agricultural commodity,   (1) for the purpose of assisting any such association in the acquisition, by purchase, construction, or otherwise, of facilities to be used in the storage, processing, or sale of such agricultural commodity, or   (2) for the purpose of furnishing funds to such associations for necessary expenditures in federating, consolidating, or merging cooperative associations, or   (3) for the purpose of furnishing to any such association funds to be used by it as capital for any agricultural credit corporation eligible for receiving rediscounts from an intermediate-credit bank. . .

(d)   The board may at any time enter into a contract with any cooperative marketing association engaged in marketing any basic agricultural commodity, insuring such association for periods of 12 months against decline in the market price for such commodity at the market price for such commodity at the time of delivery to the association. . . .

McNARY-HAUGEN BILL VETO
February 25, 1927

In May, 1928, President Coolidge again vetoed another version of the bill for agricultural relief.

To the Senate:

The conditions which Senate bill 4803 is designed to remedy have been, and still are, unsatisfactory in many cases. No one can deny that the prices of many farm products have been out of line with the general price level for several years. No one could fail to want every proper step taken to assure to agriculture a just and secure place in our economic scheme. Reasonable and constructive legislation to that end would be thoroughly justified and would have the hearty support of all who have the interests of the Nation at heart. The difficulty with this particular measure is that it is not framed to aid farmers as a whole, and it is, furthermore, calculated to injure rather than promote the general public welfare.

It is axiomatic that progress is made through building on the good foundations that already exist. For many years – indeed, from before the day of modern agricultural science – balanced and diversified farming has been regarded by thoughtful farmers and scientists as the safeguard of our agriculture. The bill under consideration throws this aside as of no consequence. It says in effect that all the agricultural scientists and all the thinking farmers of the last 50 years are wrong, that what we ought to do is not to encourage diversified agriculture but instead put a premium on one-crop farming.

The measure discriminates definitely against products which make up what has been universally considered a program of safe farming. The bill upholds as ideals of American farming the men who grow cotton, corn, rice, swine, tobacco, or wheat, and nothing else. These are to be given special favors at the expense of the farmer who has toiled for years to build up a constructive farming enterprise to include a variety of crops and livestock that shall, so far as possible, be safe, and keep the soil, the farmer's chief asset, fertile and productive.

The bill singles out a few products, chiefly sectional, and proposes to raise the prices of those regardless of the fact that thousands of other farmers would be directly penalized. . . . So far as the farmers as a whole are concerned this measure is not for them. . . .

This measure provides specifically for the payment by the Federal board of all losses, costs, and charges of packers, millers, cotton spinners, or other processors who are operating under contract with the board. It contemplates that the packers may be commissioned by the Government to buy hogs enough to create a near scarcity in this country, slaughter the hogs, sell the pork products abroad at a loss, and have their losses, costs, and charges made good out of the pockets of farm taxpayers. The millers would be similarly commissioned. . . .

It seems almost incredible that the producers of hogs, corn, wheat, rice, tobacco, and cotton should be offered a scheme of legislative relief in which the only persons who are guaranteed a profit are the exporters, packers, millers, cotton spinners, and other processors.

Clearly this legislation involves government fixing of prices. It gives the proposed Federal board almost unlimited authority to fix prices on the designated commodities. This is price fixing, furthermore, on some of the Nation's basic foods and materials. Nothing is more certain that that such price fixing would upset the normal exchange relationships existing in the open market and that it would finally have to be extended to cover a multitude of other goods and services. . . .

This legislation proposes, in effect, that Congress shall delegate to a Federal Farm Board, nominated by farmers, the power to fix and collect a tax, called an equalization fee, on certain products produced by those farmers. That certainly contemplates a remarkable delegation of the taxing power. . . .

This so-called equalization fee is not a tax for purposes of revenue in the accepted sense. It is a tax for the special benefit of particular groups. . . .

The chief objection to the bill is that it would not benefit the farmer. Whatever may be the temporary influence of arbitrary interference, no one can deny that in the long run prices will be governed by the law of supply and demand. To expect to increase prices and then to maintain them on a higher level by means of a plan which must of necessity increase production while decreasing consumption, is to fly in the face of an economic law as well established as any law of nature. . . .

A board of 12 men are granted almost unlimited control of the agricultural industry and can not only fix the price which the producers of five commodities shall receive for their goods, but can also fix the price which the consumers of the country shall pay for these commodities. The board is expected to obtain higher prices for the American farmer by removing the surplus from the home market and dumping it abroad at a below-cost price. To do this, the board is given the authority by implication to fix the domestic price level, either by means of contracts which it may make with processors or cooperatives, or by providing for the purchase of the commodities in such quantities as will bring the prices up to the point which the board may fix.

Except as it may be restrained by fear of foreign importations, the farm board, composed of representatives of producers, is given the power to fix the prices of these necessities of life at any point it sees fit. The law fixes no standards, imposes no restrictions, and requires no regulation of any kind. There could be no appeal from the arbitrary decision of these men, who would be under constant pressure from their constituents to push prices as high as possible. . . . The granting of any such arbitrary power to a Government board is to run counter to our traditions, the philosophy of our Government, the spirit of our institutions, and all principles of equity.

The administrative difficulties involved are sufficient to wreck the plan. . . . How can the board be expected to carry out after the enactment of the law what can not even be described prior to its passage? In the meanwhile, existing channels and methods of distribution and marketing must be seriously dislocated.

This is even more apparent when we take into consideration the problem of administering the collection of the equalization fee. The bureau states that the fee will have to be collected either from the processors or the transportation companies, and dismisses as impracticable collections at the point of sale. In the case of transportation companies it points out the enormous difficulties of collecting the fee in view of the possibility of shipping commodities by unregistered vehicles. In so far as processors are concerned, it estimates the number at 6,632, without considering the number of factories engaged in the business of canning corn or manufacturing food products other than millers. Some conception of the magnitude of the task may be had when we consider that if the wheat, the corn, and the cotton crops had been under operation in the year 1925, collection would have been required from an aggregate of 16,034,466.679 units. The bureau states that it will be impossible to collect the equalization fee in full.

The bill will not succeed in providing a practical method of controlling the agricultural surplus, which lies at the heart of the whole problem. In the matter of controlling output, the farmer is at a disadvantage as compared with the manufacturer. The latter is better able to gauge his market, and in the face of falling prices can reduce production. The farmer, on the other hand, must operate over a longer period of time in producing his crops and is subject to weather conditions and disturbances in world markets which can never be known in advance. In trying to find a solution for this fundamental problem of the surplus, the present bill offers no constructive suggestion. It seeks merely to increase the prices paid by the consumer, with the inevitable result of stimulating production on the part of the farmer and decreasing consumption on the part of the public. It ignores the fact that production is curbed only by decreased, not increased, prices. . . .

We must be careful in trying to help the farmer not to jeopardize the whole agricultural industry by subjecting it to the tyranny of bureaucratic regulation and control. That is what the present bill will do. But aside from all this, no man can foresee what the effect on our economic life will be of disrupting the long-established and delicately adjusted channels of commerce. . . .

The effect of this plan will be continuously to stimulate American production and to pile up increasing surpluses beyond the world demand. . . .

FIFTH ANNUAL MESSAGE
December 6, 1927

Three important events in United States foreign relations—endangerment of American lives and property in Mexico, and the sending of troops to protect United States citizens in China and Nicaragua — received relatively small space in the President's message. He continued to stress the need to reduce both taxes and national debt.

Members of the Congress:

It is gratifying to report that for the fourth consecutive year the state of the Union in general is good. . . .

CONSTRUCTIVE ECONOMY

Without constructive economy in Government expenditures we should not now be enjoying these results or these prospects. Because we are not now physically at war, some people are disposed to forget that our war debt still remains. The Nation must make financial sacrifices, accompanied by a stern self-denial in public expenditures, until we have conquered the disabilities of our public finance. While our obligation to veterans and dependents is large and continuing, the heavier burden of the national debt is being steadily eliminated. At the end of this fiscal year it will be reduced from about $26,600,-000,000 to about $17,975,000,000. Annual interest, including war savings, will have been reduced from $1,055,000,000 to $670,000,000. The sacrifices of the people, the economy of the Government, are showing remarkable results. They should be continued for the purpose of relieving the Nation of the burden of interest and debt and releasing revenue for internal improvements and national development.

Not only the amount, but the rate, of Government interest has been reduced. Callable bonds have been refunded and paid, so that during this year the average rate of interest on the present public debt for the first time fell below 4 per cent. Keeping the credit of the Nation high is a tremendously profitable operation.

TAX REDUCTION

The immediate fruit of economy and the retirement of the public debt is tax reduction. The annual saving in interest between 1925 and 1929 is $212,000,000. Without this no bill to relieve the taxpayers would be worth proposing. The three measures already enacted leave our Government revenues where they are not oppressive. Exemptions have been increased until 115,000,000 people make but 2,500,000 individual taxable returns, so that further reduction should be mainly for the purpose of removing inequalities. The Secretary of the Treasury has recommended a measure which would give us a much better balanced system of taxation and without oppression produce sufficient revenue. It has my complete support.

Unforeseen contingencies requiring money are always arising. Our probable surplus for June 30, 1929, is small. A slight depression in business would greatly reduce our revenue because of our present method of taxation. The people ought to take no selfish attitude of pressing for removing moderate and fair taxes which might produce a deficit. We must keep our budget balanced for each year. That is the corner stone of our national credit, the trifling price we pay to command the lowest rate of interest of any great power in the world. Any surplus can be applied to debt reduction, and debt reduction is tax reduction. Under the present circumstances it would be far better to leave the rates as they are than to enact a bill carrying the peril of a deficit. This is not a problem to be approached in a narrow or partisan spirit. All of those who participate in finding a reasonable solution will be entitled to participate in any credit that accrues from it without regard to party. The Congress has already demonstrated that tax legislation can be removed from purely political consideration into the realm of patriotic business principles.

Any bill for tax reduction should be written by those who are responsible for raising, managing, and expending the finances of the Government. If special interests, too often selfish, always uninformed of the national needs as a whole, with hired agents using their proposed beneficiaries as engines of propaganda, are permitted to influence the withdrawal of their property from taxation, we shall have a law that is unbalanced and unjust, bad for business, bad for the country, probably resulting in a deficit, with disastrous financial consequences. The Constitution has given the Members of the Congress sole authority to decide what tax measures shall be presented for approval. While welcoming information from any quarter, the Congress should continue to exercise its own judgment in a matter as vital and important to all the interests of the country as taxation.

NATIONAL DEFENSE

. . . Our Navy is likewise a weapon of defense. We have a foreign commerce and ocean lines of trade unsurpassed by any other country. We have outlying territory in the two great oceans and long stretches of seacoast studded with the richest cities in the world. We are responsible for the protection of a large population and the greatest treasure ever bestowed upon any people. We are charged with an international duty of defending the Panama Canal. To meet these responsibilities we need a very substantial sea armament. It needs airplane carriers and a material addition to its force of cruisers. We can plan for the future and begin a moderate building program.

This country has put away the Old World policy of competitive armaments. It can never be relieved of the responsibility of adequate national defense. We have one treaty secured by an unprecedented attitude of generosity on our part for a limitation in naval armament. After most careful preparation, extending over months, we recently made every effort to secure a three-power treaty to the same end. We were granted much cooperation by Japan, but we were unable to come to an agreement with Great Britain. While the results of the conference were of considerable value, they were mostly of a negative character. We know now that no agreement can be reached which will be inconsistent with a considerable building program on our part. We are ready and willing to continue the preparatory investigations on the general subject of limitation of armaments which have been started under the auspices of the League of Nations. . . .

MERCHANT MARINE

The United States Government fleet is transporting a large amount of freight and reducing its drain on the Treasury. The Shipping Board is constantly under pressure, to which it too often yields, to protect private interests, rather than serve the public welfare. More attention should be given to merchant ships as an auxiliary of the Navy. . . .

COMMERCIAL AVIATION

A rapid growth is taking place in aeronautics. The Department of Commerce has charge of the inspection and licensing system and the construction of national airways. Almost 8,000 miles are already completed and about 4,000 miles more contemplated. Nearly 4,400 miles are now equipped and over 3,000 miles more will have lighting and emergency landing fields by next July. Air mail contracts are expected to cover 24 of these lines. Daily airway flying is nearly 15,000 miles and is expected to reach 25,000 miles early next year.

Flights for other purposes exceed 22,000 miles each day. Over 900 airports, completed and uncompleted, have been laid out. The demand for aircraft has greatly increased. The policy already adopted by the Congress is producing the sound development of this coming industry.

WESTERN HEMISPHERE AIR MAIL

Private enterprise is showing much interest in opening up aviation service to Mexico and Central and South America. We are particularly solicitous to have the United States take a leading part in this development. It is understood that the governments of our sister countries would be willing to cooperate. Their physical features, the undeveloped state of their transportation, make an air service especially adaptable to their usage. The Post Office Department should be granted power to make liberal long-term contracts for carrying our mail, and authority should be given to the Army and the Navy to detail aviators and planes to cooperate with private enterprise in establishing such mail service with the consent of the countries concerned. A committee of the Cabinet will later present a report on this subject.

GOOD ROADS

The importance and benefit of good roads is more and more coming to be appreciated. The National Government has been making liberal contributions to encourage their construction. The results and benefits have been very gratifying. National participation, however, should be confined to trunk-line systems. . . .

While the advantage of having good roads is very large, the desire for improved highways is not limited to our own country. It should and does include all the Western Hemisphere. The principal points in Canada are already accessible. We ought to lend our encouragement in any way we can for more good roads to all the principal points in this hemisphere south of the Rio Grande. . . .

CUBAN PARCEL POST

We have a temporary parcel-post convention with Cuba. The advantage of it is all on our side. During 1926 we shipped twelve times as many parcels, weighing twenty-four times as much, as we received. This convention was made on the understanding that we would repeal an old law prohibiting the importation of cigars and cigarettes in quantities less than 3,000 enacted in 1866 to discourage smuggling, for which it has long been unnecessary. This law unjustly discriminates against an important industry of Cuba. Its repeal has been recommended by the Treasury and Post Office Departments. . . .

Conditions in the Philippine Islands have been steadily improved. Contentment and good order prevail. Roads, irrigation works, harbor improvements, and public buildings are being constructed. Public education and sanitation have been advanced. The Government is in a sound financial condition. These immediate results were especially due to the administration of Gov. Gen. Leonard Wood. . . . His death is a loss to the Nation and the islands. . . .

A fair degree of progress is being made in Porto Rico. Its agricultural products are increasing; its treasury position, which has given much concern, shows improvement. I am advised by the governor that educational facilities are still lacking. Roads are being constructed, which he represents are the first requisite for building schoolhouses. The loyalty of the island to the United States is exceedingly gratifying. A memorial will be presented to you requesting authority to have the governor elected by the people of Porto Rico. This was never done in the case of our own Territories. . . .

PANAMA CANAL

The number of commercial ships passing through the Panama Canal has increased from 3,967 in 1923 to 5,475 in 1927. The total amount of tolls turned into the Treasury is over $166,000,000, while all the operations of the canal have yielded a surplus of about $80,000-000. . . .

AGRICULTURE

The past year has seen a marked improvement in the general condition of agriculture. Production is better balanced and without acute shortage or heavy surplus. . . .

Agriculture has not fully recovered from postwar depression. The fact is that economic progress never marches forward in a straight line. It goes in waves. . . .

In the past the Government has spent vast sums to bring land under cultivation. It is apparent that this has reached temporarily the saturation point. We have had a surplus of production and a poor market for land, which has only lately shown signs of improvement. The main problem which is presented for solution is one of dealing with a surplus of production. It is useless to propose a temporary expedient. What is needed is permanency and stability. Government price fixing is known to be unsound and bound to result in disaster. A Government subsidy would work out in the same way. It can not be sound for all of the people to hire some of the people to produce a crop which neither the producers nor the rest of the people want.

Price fixing and subsidy will both increase the surplus, instead of diminishing it. Putting the Government directly into business is merely a combination of subsidy and price fixing aggravated by political pressure. These expedients would lead logically to telling the farmer by law what and how much he should plant and where he should plant it, and what and how much he should sell and where he should sell it. The most effective means of dealing with surplus crops is to reduce the surplus acreage. While this can not be done by the individual farmer, it can be done through the organizations already in existence, through the information published by the Department of Agriculture, and especially through banks and others who supply credit refusing to finance an acreage manifestly too large.

It is impossible to provide by law for an assured success and prosperity for all those who engage in farming. If acreage becomes overextended, the Government can not assume responsibility for it. The Government can, however, assist cooperative associations and other organizations in orderly marketing and handling a surplus clearly due to weather and seasonal conditions, in order to save the producer from preventable loss. While it is probably impossible to secure this result at a single step, and much will have to be worked out by trial and rejection, a beginning could be made by setting up a Federal board or commission of able and experienced men in marketing, granting equal advantages under this board to the various agricultural commodities and sections of the country, giving encouragement to the cooperative movement in agriculture, and providing a revolving loan fund at a moderate rate of interest for the necessary financing. Such legislation would lay the foundation for a permanent solution of the surplus problem.

This is not a proposal to lend more money to the farmer, who is already fairly well financed, but to lend money temporarily to experimental marketing associations which will no doubt ultimately be financed by the regularly established banks, as were the temporary operations of the War Finance Corporation. Cooperative marketing especially would be provided with means of buying or building physical properties.

The National Government has almost entirely relieved the farmer from income taxes by successive tax reductions, but State and local taxes have increased, putting on him a grievous burden. A policy of rigid economy should be applied to State and local expenditures. This is clearly within the legislative domain of the States. . . .

. . . It is often stated that a reduction of tariff rates on industry would benefit agriculture. It would be interesting to know to what commodities it is thought this could be applied. Everything the farmer uses in farming is already on the free list. Nearly everything he sells

is protected. It would seem to be obvious that it is better for the country to have the farmer raise food to supply the domestic manufacturer
than the foreign manufacturer. . . .

FARM LOAN SYSTEM

It is exceedingly important that the Federal land and joint-stock
land banks should furnish the best possible service for agriculture.
Certain joint-stock banks have fallen into improper and unsound prac-
tices, resulting in the indictment of the officials of three of them.
More money has been provided for examinations, and at the instance
of the Treasury rules and regulations of the Federal Farm Board have
been revised. Early last May three of its members resigned. Their
places were filled with men connected with the War Finance Corporation, Eugene Meyer being designated as Farm Loan Commissioner.
The new members have demonstrated their ability in the field of agricultural finance in the extensive operations of the War Finance Corporation. Three joint-stock banks have gone into receivership. It is
necessary to preserve the public confidence in this system in order
to find a market for their bonds. A recent flotation was made at a
record low rate of 4 per cent. Careful supervision is absolutely necessary to protect the investor and enable these banks to exercise their
chief function in serving agriculture.

MUSCLE SHOALS

The last year has seen considerable changes in the problem of
Muscle Shoals. Development of other methods show that nitrates can
probably be produced at less cost than by the use of hydro-electric
power. Extensive investigation made by the Department of War indicates that the nitrate plants on this project are of little value for
national defense and can probably be disposed of within two years. The
oxidation part of the plants, however, should be retained indefinitely.
This leaves this project mostly concerned with power. It should,
nevertheless, continue to be dedicated to agriculture. It is probable
that this desire can be best served by disposing of the plant and applying the revenues received from it to research for methods of more
economical production of concentrated fertilizer and to demonstrations
and other methods of stimulating its use on the farm. But in disposing
of the property preference should be given to proposals to use all or
part of it for nitrate production and fertilizer manufacturing.

FLOOD CONTROL

For many years the Federal Government has been building a system
of dikes along the Mississippi River for protection against high water.
During the past season the lower States were overcome by a most dis-

astrous flood. Many thousands of square miles were inundated, a great many lives were lost, much livestock was drowned, and a very heavy destruction of property was inflicted upon the inhabitants. The American Red Cross at once went to the relief of the stricken communities. Appeals for contributions have brought in over $17,000,000. The Federal Government has provided services, equipment, and supplies probably amounting to about $7,000,000 more. Between $5,000,000 and $10,000,000 in addition have been provided by local railroads, the States, and their political units. Credits have been arranged by the Farm Loan Board, and three emergency finance corporations with a total capital of $3,000,000 have insured additional resources to the extent of $12,000,000. Through these means the 700,000 people in the flooded areas have been adequately supported. Provision has been made to care for those in need until after the 1st of January.

The Engineer Corps of the Army has contracted to close all breaks in the dike system before the next season of high water. A most thorough and elaborate survey of the whole situation has been made and embodied in a report with recommendations for future flood control, which will be presented to the Congress. The carrying out of their plans will necessarily extend over a series of years. They will call for a raising and strengthening of the dike system with provision for emergency spillways and improvements for the benefit of navigation. . . .

Legislation by this Congress should be confined to our principal and most pressing problem, the lower Mississippi, considering tributaries only so far as they materially affect the main flood problem. A definite Federal program relating to our waterways was proposed when the last Congress authorized a comprehensive survey of all the important streams of the country in order to provide for their improvement, including flood control, navigation, power, and irrigation. Other legislation should wait pending a report on this survey. . . .

INLAND NAVIGATION

The Congress in its last session authorized the general improvements necessary to provide the Mississippi waterway system with better transportation. Stabilization of the levels of the Great Lakes and their opening to the sea by an effective shipway remain to be considered. Since the last session the Board of Engineers of the War Department has made a report on the proposal for a canal through the State of New York, and the Joint Board of Engineers, representing Canada and the United States, has finished a report on the St. Lawrence River. Both of these boards conclude that the St. Lawrence project is cheaper, affords a more expeditious method of placing western products in European markets, and will cost less to operate. The State Department has requested the Canadian Government to negotiate treaties necessary to provide for this improvement. It will also be necessary to secure an agreement with Canada to put in works necessary to prevent fluctuation in the levels of the Great Lakes.

Legislation is desirable for the construction of a dam at Boulder Canyon on the Colorado River, primarily as a method of flood control and irrigation. A secondary result would be a considerable power development and a source of domestic water supply for southern California. Flood control is clearly a national problem, and water supply is a Government problem, but every other possibility should be exhausted before the Federal Government becomes engaged in the power business. The States which are interested ought to reach mutual agreement. This project is in reality their work. If they wish the Federal Government to undertake it, they should not hesitate to make the necessary concessions to each other. . . .

THE NEGRO

History does not anywhere record so much progress made in the same length of time as that which has been accomplished by the Negro race in the United States since the Emancipation Proclamation. . . . They have especially been made the target of the foul crime of lynching. For several years these acts of unlawful violence had been diminishing. In the last year they have shown an increase. Every principle of order and law and liberty is opposed to this crime. The Congress should enact any legislation it can under the Constitution to provide for its elimination.

AMERICAN INDIAN

The condition of the American Indian has much improved in recent years. Full citizenship was bestowed upon them on June 2, 1924, and appropriations for their care and advancement have been increased. Still there remains much to be done.

Notable increases in appropriations for the several major functions performed by the Department of the Interior on behalf of the Indians have marked the last five years. In that time, successive annual increases in appropriations for their education total $1,804,325; for medical care $578,000; and for industrial advancement, $205,000; or $2,582,325 more than would have been spent in the same period on the basis of appropriations for 1923 and the preceding years.

The needs along health, educational, industrial, and social lines, however, are great, and the Budget estimates for 1929 include still further increases for Indian administration.

To advance the time when the Indians may become self-sustaining, it is my belief that the Federal Government should continue to improve the facilities for their care, and as rapidly as possible turn its responsibility over to the States.

COAL

Legislation authorizing a system of fuel administration and the appointment by the President of a Board of Mediation and Conciliation in case of actual or threatened interruption of production is needed. The miners themselves are now seeking information and action from the Government, which could readily be secured through such a board. It is believed that a thorough investigation and reconsideration of this proposed policy by the Congress will demonstrate that this recommendation is sound and should be adopted.

PETROLEUM CONSERVATION

The National Government is undertaking to join in the formation of a cooperative committee of lawyers, engineers, and public officers, to consider what legislation by the States or by the Congress can be adopted for the preservation and conservation of our supply of petroleum. This has come to be one of the main dependencies for transportation and power so necessary to our agricultural and industrial life. It is expected the report of this committee will be available for later congressional action. Meantime, the requirement that the Secretary of the Interior should make certain leases of land belonging to the Osage Indians, in accordance with the act of March 3, 1921, should be repealed. The authority to lease should be discretionary, in order that the property of the Indians may not be wasted and the public suffer a future lack of supply.

ALIEN PROPERTY

Under treaty the property held by the Alien Property Custodian was to be retained until suitable provision had been made for the satisfaction of American claims. While still protecting the American claimants, in order to afford every possible accommodation to the nationals of the countries whose property was held, the Congress has made liberal provision for the return of a large part of the property. All trusts under $10,000 were returned in full, and partial returns were made on the others. The total returned was approximately $350,000,000.

There is still retained, however, about $250,000,000. The Mixed Claims Commission has made such progress in the adjudication of claims that legislation can now be enacted providing for the return of the property, which should be done under conditions which will protect our Government and our claimants. Such a measure will be proposed, and I recommend its enactment.

RAILROAD CONSOLIDATION

In order to increase the efficiency of transportation and decrease its cost to the shipper, railroad consolidation must be secured. Legislation is needed to simplify the necessary procedure to secure such agreements and arrangements for consolidation, always under the control and with the approval of the Interstate Commerce Commission. Pending this, no adequate or permanent reorganization can be made of the freight-rate structure. Meantime, both agriculture and industry are compelled to wait for needed relief. This is purely a business question, which should be stripped of all local and partisan bias and decided on broad principles and its merits in order to promote the public welfare. A large amount of new construction and equipment, which will furnish employment for labor and markets for commodities of both factory and farm, wait on the decision of this important question. Delay is holding back the progress of our country. . . .

VETERANS

. . . It has been suggested that the various governmental agencies now dealing with veterans' relief be consolidated. This would bring many advantages. It is recommended that the proper committees of the Congress make a thorough survey of this subject, in order to determine if legislation to secure such consolidation is desirable.

EDUCATION

For many years it has been the policy of the Federal Government to encourage and foster the cause of education. Large sums of money are annually appropriated to carry on vocational training. Many millions go into agricultural schools. The general subject is under the immediate direction of a Commissioner of Education. While this subject is strictly a State and local function, it should continue to have the encouragement of the National Government. I am still of the opinion that much good could be accomplished through the establishment of a Department of Education and Relief, into which would be gathered all of these functions under one directing member of the Cabinet.

DEPARTMENT OF LABOR

Industrial relations have never been more peaceful. In recent months they have suffered from only one serious controversy. In all others difficulties have been adjusted, both management and labor wishing to settle controversies by friendly agreement rather than by compulsion. The welfare of women and children is being especially guarded by our Department of Labor. Its Children's Bureau is in co-operation with 26 State boards and 80 juvenile courts.

Through its Bureau of Immigration it has been found that medical examination abroad has saved prospective immigrants from much hardship. Some further legislation to provide for reuniting families when either the husband or the wife is in this country, and granting more freedom for the migration of the North American Indian tribes is desirable.

The United States Employment Service has enabled about 2,000,000 men and women to gain paying positions in the last fiscal year. Particular attention has been given to assisting men past middle life and in providing field labor for harvesting agricultural crops. This has been made possible in part through the service of the Federal Board for Vocational Education, which is cooperating with the States in a program to increase the technical knowledge and skill of the wage earner.

HISTORICAL CELEBRATIONS

Provision is being made to commemorate the two hundredth anniversary of the birth of George Washington. Suggestion has been made for the construction of a memorial road leading from the Capital to Mount Vernon, which may well have the consideration of the Congress, and the commission intrusted with preparations for the celebration will undoubtedly recommend publication of the complete writings of Washington and a series of writings by different authors relating to him.

February 25, 1929, is the one hundred and fiftieth anniversary of the capture of Fort Sackville, at Vincennes, in the State of Indiana. This eventually brought into the Union what was known as the Northwest Territory, embracing the region north of the Ohio River between the Alleghenies and the Mississippi River. This expedition was led by George Rogers Clark. His heroic character and the importance of his victory are too little known and understood. They gave us not only this Northwest Territory but by means of that the prospect of reaching the Pacific. The State of Indiana is proposing to dedicate the site of Fort Sackville as a national shrine. The Federal Government may well make some provision for the erection under its own management of a fitting memorial at that point.

FOREIGN RELATIONS

It is the policy of the United States to promote peace. . . . We have believed that peace can best be secured by a faithful observance on our part of the principles of international law, accompanied by patience and conciliation, and requiring of others a like treatment for ourselves. We have lately had some difference with Mexico relative to the injuries inflicted upon our nationals and their property within that country. A firm adherence to our rights and a scrupulous respect for the sovereignty of Mexico, both in accordance with the law of nations, coupled with patience and forbearance, it is hoped will resolve all our differences without interfering with the friendly relationship between the two Governments.

We have been compelled to send naval and marine forces to China to protect the lives and property of our citizens. Fortunately their simple presence there has been sufficient to prevent any material loss of life. But there has been considerable loss of property. That unhappy country is torn by factions and revolutions which bid fair to last for an indefinite period. Meanwhile we are protecting our citizens and stand ready to cooperate with any government which may emerge in promoting the welfare of the people of China. They have always had our friendship, and they should especially merit our consideration in these days of their distraction and distress.

We were confronted by similar condition on a small scale in Nicaragua. Our marine and naval forces protected our citizens and their property and prevented a heavy sacrifice of life and the destruction of that country by a reversion to a state of revolution. Henry L. Stimson, former Secretary of War, was sent there to cooperate with our diplomatic and military officers in effecting a settlement between the contending parties. This was done on the assurance that we would cooperate in restoring a state of peace where our rights would be protected by giving our assistance in the conduct of the next presidential election, which occurs in a few months. With this assurance the population returned to their peace-time pursuits, with the exception of some small roving bands of outlaws.

In general, our relations with other countries can be said to have improved within the year. . . .

AMERICAN PROGRESS

Our country has made much progress. But it has taken, and will continue to take, much effort. Competition will be keen, the temptation to selfishness and arrogance will be severe, the provocations to deal harshly with weaker peoples will be many. All of these are embraced in the opportunity for true greatness. They will be overbalanced by cooperation, by generosity, and a spirit of neighborly kindness. The forces of the universe are taking humanity in that direction. In doing good, in walking humbly, in sustaining its own people, in ministering to other nations, America will work out its own mighty destiny.

SECOND McNARY-HAUGEN VETO
May, 1928

The farm bloc's efforts to have the McNary-Haugen pro-
posals enacted into law had consistently roused the strong
opposition of Coolidge. In this veto, his language went
far beyond his usual reserved words.

Senate bill 3555, called the Surplus Control Act, is in some respects an improvement over Senate Bill 4808 of the last Congress. It includes several provisions which, if unencumbered by objectionable features, would form a basis for a measure that should do much to develop stronger business organizations in agriculture. But the present bill contains not only the so-called equalization fee and other features of the old measure prejudicial, in my opinion, to sound public policy and to agriculture, but also new and highly objectionable provisions. . . .

In its essentials the objectionable plan proposed here is the stimulation of the price of agricultural commodities and products thereof by artificially controlling the surpluses so that there will be an apparent scarcity on the market. . . .

It embodies a formidable array of perils for agriculture which are all the more menacing because of their being obscured in a maze of ponderously futile bureaucratic paraphernalia. In fact, in spite of the inclusion in this measure of some constructive steps proposed by the administration, it renews most of the more vicious devices which appeared in the bill that was vetoed last year. This document is much altered from its previous form; but its substance, particularly as to its evident ultimate effect of tending to delude the farmer with a fantastic promise of unworkable governmental price regulation, is still as repugnant as ever to the spirit of our institutions, both political and commercial.

A detailed analysis of all of the objections to the measure would involve a document of truly formidable proportions. However, its major weaknesses and perils may be summarized under six headings:

1. Its attempted price-fixing fallacy.
2. The tax characteristics of the equalization fee.
3. The widespread bureaucracy which it would set up.
4. Its encouragement to profiteering and wasteful distribution by middlemen.
5. Its stimulation of overproduction.
6. Its aid to our foreign agricultural competitions. These topics by no means exhaust the list of fallacious and indeed dangerous aspects of the bill, but they afford ample ground for its emphatic rejection.

1. Price fixing. This measure is as cruelly deceptive in its disguise as governmental price-fixing legislation. . . as any of the other so-called surplus control bills.

2. The equalization fee, which is the krenel of this legislation, is a sales tax upon the entire community. It is in no sense a mere contribution to be made by the producers themselves, as has been represented by supporters of the measure. It can be assessed upon the commodities in transit to the consumer and its burdens can often unmistakably be passed on to him.

Furthermore, such a procedure would certainly involve an extraordinary relinquishment of the taxing power on the part of Congress, because the tax would not only be levied without recourse to legislative authority but its proceeds would be expended entirely without the usual safeguards of congressional control of appropriations. This would be a most dangerous nullification of one of the essential checks and balances which lie at the very foundation of our government.

Incidentally, this taxation or fee would not be for purposes of revenue in the accepted sense but would simply yield a subsidy for the special benefit of particular groups of processors and exporters. . . . It would be difficult indeed to conceive of a more flagrant case of the employment of all of the coercive powers of the government for the profit of a small number of specially privileged groups. . . .

3. Widespread bureaucracy. A bureaurcratic tyranny of unprecedented proportions would be let down upon the backs of the farm industry and its distributors throughout the nation in connection with the enforcement of this measure. . . .

KELLOGG-BRIAND PACT
August 27, 1928

A France-United States agreement to outlaw war was pro-
posed on April 6, 1927, by Aristide Briand, French foreign
minister. It has been suggested by Professor James T.
Shotwell of Columbia University. On December 28, 1927,
U.S. Secretary of State Frank B. Kellogg proposed that
the agreement be extended to the major world powers.
Fifteen signed initially in Paris; ultimately 62 nations
signed the treaty. Kellogg received the Nobel Peace Prize
in 1929 for his part in the effort.

The President of the German Reich, the President of the United
States of America, His Majesty the King of the Belgians, the President
of the French Republic, His Majesty the King of Great Britain, Irel-
land and the British Dominions beyond the seas, Emperor of India,
His Majesty the King of Italy, His Majesty the Emperor of Japan, the
President of the Republic of Poland, the President of the Czechoslovak
Republic, . . . deeply sensible of their solemn duty to promote the
welfare of mankind;

Persuaded that the time has come when a frank renunciation of
war as an instrument of national policy should be made to the end that
the peaceful and friendly relations now existing between their peoples
may be perpetuated;

Convinced that all changes in their relations with one another should
be sought only by pacific means and be the result of a peaceful and
orderly process, and that any signatory Power which shall hereafter
seek to promote its national interests by resort to war should be
denied the benefits furnished by this Treaty;

Hopeful that, encouraged by their example, all the other nations
of the world will join in this humane endeavour and by adhering to the
present Treaty as soon as it comes into force bring their peoples
within the scope of its beneficent provisions, thus uniting the civilized
nations of the world in a common renunciation of war as an instrument
of their national policy;

Have decided to conclude a Treaty. . . .

ARTICLE I.

The High Contracting Parties solemnly declare in the names of
their respective peoples that they condemn recourse to war for the
solution of international controversies, and renounce it as an instrument of national policy in their relations with one another.

ARTICLE II.

The High Contracting Parties agree that the settlement or solution of all disputes or conflicts of whatever nature or of whatever origin they may be, which may arise among them, shall never be sought except by pacific means.

ARTICLE III.

The present Treaty shall be ratified by the High Contracting Parties names in the Preamble in accordance with their respective constitutional requirements, and shall take effect as between them as soon as all their several instruments of ratification shall have been deposited at Washington.

This Treaty shall, when it has come into effect as prescribed in the preceding paragraph, remain open as long as may be necessary for adherence by all the other Powers of the world. . . .

SIXTH ANNUAL MESSAGE
December 4, 1928

Coolidge's final annual message to Congress drew a picture of a prosperous, forward-moving nation under an efficient administration — a picture to be shattered by the economic events of the succeeding year.

To the Congress of the United States:

No Congress of the United States ever assembled, on surveying the state of the Union, has met with a more pleasing prospect than that which appears at the present time. In the domestic field there is tranquillity and contentment, harmonious relations between management and wage earner, freedom from industrial strife, and the highest record of years of prosperity. In the foreign field there is peace, the good will which comes from mutual understanding, and the knowledge that the problems which a short time ago appeared so ominous are yielding to the touch of manifest friendship. The great wealth created by our enterprise and industry, and saved by our economy, has had the widest distribution among our own people, and has gone out in a steady stream to serve the charity and the business of the world. The requirements of existence have passed beyond the standard of necessity into the region of luxury. Enlarging production is consumed by an increasing demand at home and an expanding commerce abroad. The country can regard the present with satisfaction and anticipate the future with optimism.

The main source of these unexampled blessings lies in the integrity and character of the American people. They have had great faith, which they have supplemented with mighty works. They have been able to put trust in each other and trust in their Government. Their candor in dealing with foreign governments has commanded respect and confidence. Yet these remarkable powers would have been exerted almost in vain without the constant cooperation and careful administration of the Federal Government.

We have been coming into a period which may be fairly characterized as a conservation of our national resources. Wastefulness in public business and private enterprise has been displaced by constructive economy. This has been accomplished by bringing our domestic and foreign relations more and more under a reign of law. A rule of force has been giving way to a rule of reason. We have substituted for the vicious circle of increasing expenditures, increasing tax rates, and diminishing profits the charmed circle of diminishing expenditures, diminishing tax rates, and increasing profits.

Four times we have made a drastic revision of our internal revenue system, abolishing many taxes and substantially reducing almost all others. Each time the resulting stimulation to business has so increased taxable incomes and profits that a surplus has been produced. One-third of the national debt has been paid, while much of the other two-thirds has been refunded at lower rates, and these savings of interest and constant economies have enabled us to repeat the satisfying process of more tax reductions. Under this sound and healthful encouragement the national income has increased nearly 50 per cent, until it is estimated to stand well over $90,000,000,000. It has been a method which has performed the seeming miracle of leaving a much greater percentage of earnings in the hands of the taxpayers with scarcely any diminution of the Government revenue. That is constructive economy in the highest degree. It is the corner stone of prosperity. It should not fail to be continued.

This action began by the application of economy to public expenditure. If it is to be permanent, it must be made so by the repeated application of economy. There is no surplus on which to base further tax revision at this time. Last June the estimates showed a threatened deficit for the current fiscal year of $94,000,000. Under my direction the departments began saving all they could out of their present appropriations. The last tax reduction brought an encouraging improvement in business, beginning early in October, which will also increase our revenue. The combination of economy and good times now indicates a surplus of about $37,000,000. This is a margin of less than 1 per cent on our expenditures and makes it obvious that the Treasury is in no condition to undertake increases in expenditures to be made before June 30. It is necessary therefore during the present session to refrain from new appropriations for immediate outlay, or if such are absolutely required to provide for them by new revenue; otherwise, we shall reach the end of the year with the unthinkable result of an unbalanced budget. For the first time during my term of office we face that contingency. I am certain that the Congress would not pass and I should not feel warranted in approving legislation which would involve us in that financial disgrace. . . .

FOREIGN RELATIONS

When we turn from our domestic affairs to our foreign relations, we likewise perceive peace and progress. The Sixth International Conference of American States was held at Habana last winter. It contributed to a better understanding and cooperation among the nations. Eleven important conventions were signed and 71 resolutions passed. Pursuant to the plan then adopted, this Government has invited the other 20 nations of this hemisphere to a conference on conciliation and arbitration, which meets in Washington on December 10. All the nations have accepted and the expectation is justified that important progress will be made in methods for resolving international differences by means of arbitration.

During the year we have signed 11 new arbitration treaties, and 22 more are under negotiation.

NICARAGUA

When a destructive and bloody revolution lately broke out in Nicaragua, at the earnest and repeated entreaties of its Government I dispatched our Marine forces there to protect the lives and interests of our citizens. To compose the contending parties, I sent there Col. Henry L. Stimson, former Secretary of War and now Governor General of the Philippine Islands, who secured an agreement that warfare should cease, a national election should be held and peace should be restored. Both parties conscientiously carried out this agreement, with the exception of a few bandits who later mostly surrendered or left the country. President Diaz appointed Brig. Gen. Frank R. McCoy, United States Army, president of the election board, which included also one member of each political party.

A free and fair election has been held and has worked out so successfully that both parties have joined in requesting like cooperation from this country at the election four years hence, to which I have refrained from making any commitments, although our country must be gratified at such an exhibition of success and appreciation. Nicaragua is regaining its prosperity and has taken a long step in the direction of peaceful self-government.

TACNA-ARICA

The long-standing differences between Chile and Peru have been sufficiently composed so that diplomatic relations have been resumed by the exchange of ambassadors. Negotiations are hopefully proceeding as this is written for the final adjustment of the differences over their disputed territory.

MEXICO

Our relations with Mexico are on a more satisfactory basis than at any time since their revolution. Many misunderstandings have been resolved and the most frank and friendly negotiations promise a final adjustment of all unsettled questions. It is exceedingly gratifying that Ambassador Morrow has been able to bring our two neighboring countries, which have so many interests in common, to a position of confidence in each other and of respect for mutual sovereign rights.

CHINA

The situation in China which a few months ago was so threatening as to call for the dispatch of a large additional force has been much composed. The Nationalist Government has established itself over the country and promulgated a new organic law announcing a program intended to promote the political and economic welfare of the people. We have recognized this Government, encouraged its progress, and have negotiated a treaty restoring to China complete tariff autonomy and guaranteeing our citizens against discriminations. Our trade in that quarter is increasing and our forces are being reduced. . . .

PEACE TREATY

One of the most important treaties ever laid before the Senate of the United States will be that which the 15 nations recently signed at Paris, and to which 44 other nations have declared their intention to adhere, renouncing war as a national policy and agreeing to resort only to peaceful means for the adjustment of international differences. It is the most solemn declaration against war, the most positive adherence to peace, that it is possible for sovereign nations to make. It does not supersede our inalienable sovereign right and duty of national defense or undertake to commit us before the event to any mode of action which the Congress might decide to be wise if ever the treaty should be broken. But it is a new standard in the world around which can rally the informed and enlightened opinion of nations to prevent their governments from being forced into hostile action by the temporary ourbreak of international animosities. The observance of this covenant, so simple and so straight-forward, promises more for the peace of the world than any other agreement ever negotiated among the nations.

NATIONAL DEFENSE

. . . The cost of national defense is stupendous. It has increased $118,000,000 in the past four years. The estimated expenditure for 1930 is $668,000,000. While this is made up of many items it is, after all, mostly dependent upon numbers. Our defensive needs do not call for any increase in the number of men in the Army or the Navy. We have reached the limit of what we ought to expend for that purpose.

I wish to repeat again for the benefit of the timid and the suspicious that this country is neither militaristic nor imperialistic. Many people at home and abroad, who constantly make this charge, are the same ones who are even more solicitous to have us extend assistance to foreign countries. When such assistance is granted, the inevitable result is that we have foreign interests. For us to refuse the customary support and protection of such interests would be in derogation of the sovereignty of this Nation. Our largest foreign interests are in the British Empire, France, and Italy. Because we are constantly solicitous for those interests, I doubt if anyone would suppose that those countries feel we harbor toward them any militaristic or imperialistic design. As for smaller countries, we certainly do not want any of them. We are more anxious than they are to have their sovereignty respected. Our entire influence is in behalf of their independence. Cuba stands as a witness to our adherence to this principle. . . .

VETERANS

The magnitude of our present system of veterans' relief is without precedent, and the results have been far-reaching. . . . It is the conception of our Government that the pension roll is an honor roll. It should include all those who are justly entitled to its benefits, but exclude all others.

Annual expenditures for all forms of veterans' relief now approximate $765,000,000, and are increasing from year to year. It is doubtful if the peak of expenditures will be reached even under present legislation for some time yet to come. Further amendments to the existing law will be suggested by the American Legion, the Veterans of Foreign Wars of the United States, the Disabled American Veterans of the

World War, and other like organizations, and it may be necessary for administrative purposes, or in order to remove some existing inequalities in the present law, to make further changes. I am sure that such recommendations as may be submitted to the Congress will receive your careful consideration. But because of the vast expenditure now being made each year, with every assurance that it will increase, and because of the great liberality of the existing law, the proposal of any additional legislation dealing with this subject should receive most searching scrutiny from the Congress.

You are familiar with the suggestion that the various public agencies now dealing with matters of veterans' relief be consolidated in one Government department. Some advantages to this plan seem apparent, especially in the simplification of administration and in the opportunity of bringing about a greater uniformity in the application of veterans' relief. I recommend that a survey be made by the proper committees of Congress dealing with this subject, in order to determine whether legislation to secure this consolidation is desirable.

AGRICULTURE

The past year has been marked by notable though not uniform improvement in agriculture. The general purchasing power of farm products and the volume of production have advanced. . . .

In the past eight years more constructive legislation of direct benefit to agriculture has been adopted than during any other period. The Department of Agriculture has been broadened and reorganized to insure greater efficiency. The department is laying greater stress on the economic and business phases of agriculture. It is lending every possible assistance to cooperative marketing associations. Regulatory and research work have been segregated in order that each field may be served more effectively. . . .

THE SURPLUS PROBLEM

While these developments in fundamental research, regulation, and dissemination of agricultural information are of distinct help to agriculture, additional effort is needed. The surplus problem demands attention. As emphasized in my last message, the Government should assume no responsibility in normal times for crop surplus clearly due to overextended acreage. The Government should, however, provide reliable information as a guide to private effort; and in this connection fundamental research on prospective supply and demand, as a guide to production and marketing, should be encouraged. Expenditure of public funds to bring in more new land should have most searching scrutiny, so long as our farmers face unsatisfactory prices for crops and livestock produced on land already under cultivation. . . .

THE RESPONSIBILITY OF THE STATES

Important phases of public policy related to agriculture lie within the sphere of the States. While successive reductions in Federal taxes have relieved most farmers of direct taxes to the National Government, State and local levies have become a serious burden. This problem needs immediate and thorough study with a view to correction at the earliest possible moment. It will have to be made largely by the States themselves.

COMMERCE

It is desirable that the Government continue its helpful attitude toward American business. The activities of the Department of Commerce have contributed largely to the present satisfactory position in our international trade, which has reached about $9,000,000,000 annually. There should be no slackening of effort in that direction. It is also important that the department's assistance to domestic commerce be continued. There is probably no way in which the Government can aid sound economic progress more effectively than by cooperating with our business men to reduce wastes in distribution.

COMMERCIAL AERONAUTICS

Continued progress in civil aviation is most gratifying. Demands for airplanes and motors have taxed both the industry and the licensing and inspection service of the Department of Commerce to their capacity. While the compulsory licensing provisions of the air commerce act apply only to equipment and personnel engaged in interstate and foreign commerce, a Federal license may be procured by anyone possessing the necessary qualifications. State legislation, local airport regulations, and insurance requirements make such a license practically indispensable. This results in uniformity of regulation and increased safety in operation, which are essential to aeronautical development. Over 17,000 young men and women have now applied for Federal air-pilot's licenses or permits. More than 80 per cent of them applied during the past year.

Our national airway system exceeds 14,000 miles in length and has 7,500 miles lighted for night operations. Provision has been made for lighting 4,000 miles more during the current fiscal year and equipping an equal mileage with radio facilities. Three-quarters of our people are now served by these routes. With the rapid growth of air mail, express, and passenger service, this new transportation medium is daily becoming a more important factor in commerce. It is noteworthy that this development has taken place without governmental subsidies. Commercial passenger flights operating on schedule have reached 13,000 miles per day. . . .

"MAINE" BATTLESHIP MEMORIAL

When I attended the Pan American Conference at Habana, the President of Cuba showed me a marble statue made from the original memorial that was overturned by a storm after it was erected on the Cuban shore to the memory of the men who perished in the destruction of the battleship Maine. As a testimony of friendship and appreciation of the Cuban Government and people he most generously offered to present this to the United States, and I assured him of my pleasure in accepting it. There is no location in the White House for placing so large and ·heavy a structure, and I therefore urge the Congress to provide by law for some locality where it can be set up.

RAILROADS

In previous annual messages I have suggested the enactment of laws to promote railroad consolidation with the view of increasing the efficiency of transportation and lessening its cost to the public. While consolidations can and should be made under the present law until it is changed, yet the provisions of the act of 1920 have not been found fully adequate to meet the needs of other methods of consolidation. Amendments designed to remedy these defects have been considered at length by the respective committees of Congress and a bill was reported out late in the last session which I understand has the approval in principle of the Interstate Commerce Commission. It is to be hoped that this legislation may be enacted at an early date.

Experience has shown that the interstate commerce law requires definition and clarification in several other respects, some of which have been pointed out by the Interstate Commerce Commission in its annual reports to the Congress. It will promote the public interest to have the Congress give early consideration to the recommendations there made.

MERCHANT MARINE

The cost of maintaining the United States Government merchant fleet has been steadily reduced. We have established American flag lines in foreign trade where they had never before existed as a means of promoting commerce and as a naval auxiliary. There have been sold to private American capital for operation within the past few years 14 of these lines, which, under the encouragement of the recent legislation passed by the Congress, give promise of continued successful operation. Additional legislation from time to time may be necessary to promote future advancement under private control.

Through the cooperation of the Post Office Department and the Shipping Board long-term contracts are being made with American steamship lines for carrying mail, which already promise the construction of 15 to 20 new vessels and the gradual reestablishment of the American merchant marine as a private enterprise. No action of the National Government has been so beneficial to our shipping. The cost is being absorbed to a considerable extent by the disposal of unprofitable lines operated by the Shipping Board, for which the new law has made a market. Meanwhile it should be our policy to maintain necessary strategic lines under the Government operation until they can be transferred to private capital.

INTER-AMERICAN HIGHWAY

In my message last year I expressed the view that we should lend our encouragement for more good roads to all the principal points on this hemisphere south of the Rio Grande. My view has not changed. . . .

AIR MAIL SERVICE

The friendly relations and the extensive commercial intercourse with the Western Hemisphere to the south of us are being further cemented by the establishment and extension of air-mail routes. We shall soon have one from Key West, Fla., over Cuba, Haiti, and Santo Domingo to San Juan, P.R., where it will connect with another route to Trinidad. There will be another route from Key West to the Canal Zone, where connection will be made with a route across the northern coast of South America to Paramaribo. This will give us a circle around the Caribbean under our own control. Additional connections will be made at Colon with a route running down the west coast of South America as far as Concepcion, Chile, and with the French air mail at Paramaribo running down the eastern coast of South America. The air service already spans our continent, with laterals running to Mexico and Canada, and covering a daily flight of over 28,000 miles, with an average cargo of 15,000 pounds.

WATERWAYS

Our river and harbor improvements are proceeding with vigor. In the past few years we have increased the appropriation for this regular work $28,000,000, besides what is to be expended on flood control. The total appropriation for this year was over $91,000,000. The Ohio River is almost ready for opening; work on the Missouri and other rivers is under way. In accordance with the Mississippi flood law Army engineers are making investigations and surveys on other streams throughout the country with a view to flood control, navigation, waterpower, and irrigation. Our barge lines are being operated under generous appropriations, and negotiations are developing relative to the St. Lawrence waterway. To secure the largest benefits from all these waterways joint rates must be established with the railroads, preferably by agreement, but otherwise as a result of congressional action.

We have recently passed several river and harbor bills. The work ordered by the Congress, not yet completed, will cost about $243,000,-000, besides the hundreds of millions to be spent on the Mississippi flood way. Until we can see our way out of this expense no further river and harbor legislation should be passed, as expenditures to put it into effect would be four or five years away.

IRRIGATION OF ARID LANDS

For many years the Federal Government has been committed to the wise policy of reclamation and irrigation. While it has met with some failures due to unwise selection of projects and lack of thorough soil surveys, so that they could not be placed on a sound business basis, on the whole the service has been of such incalculable benefit in so many States that no one would advocate its abandonment. The program to which we are already committed, providing for the construction of new projects authorized by Congress and the completion of old projects, will tax the resources of the reclamation fund over a period of years. The high cost of improving and equipping farms adds to the difficulty of securing settlers for vacant farms on Federal projects.

Readjustments authorized by the reclamation relief act of May 25, 1926, have given more favorable terms of repayment to settlers. These new financial arrangements and the general prosperity on irrigation projects have resulted in increased collections by the Department of the Interior of charges due the reclamation fund. Nevertheless, the demand for still smaller yearly payments on some projects continues. These conditions should have consideration in connection with any proposed new projects.

COLORADO RIVER

For several years the Congress has considered the erection of a dam on the Colorado River for flood-control, irrigation, and domestic water purposes, all of which may properly be considered as Government functions. . . .

The Congress will have before it the detailed report of a special board appointed to consider the engineering and economic feasibility of this project. From the short summary which I have seen of it, I judge they consider the engineering problems can be met at somewhat increased cost over previous estimates. They prefer the Black Canyon site. On the economic features they are not so clear and appear to base their conclusions on many conditions which can not be established with certainty. So far as I can judge, however, from the summary, their conclusions appear sufficiently favorable, so that I feel warranted in recommending a measure which will protect the rights of the States, discharge the necessary Government functions, and leave the electrical field to private enterprise.

MUSCLE SHOALS

The development of other methods of producing nitrates will probably render this plant less important for that purpose than formerly. But we have it, and I am told it still provides a practical method of making nitrates for national defense and farm fertilizers. By dividing the property into its two component parts of power and nitrate plants it would be possible to dispose of the power, reserving the right to any concern that wished to make nitrates to use any power that might be needed for that purpose. Such a disposition of the power plant can be made that will return in rental about $2,000,000 per year. If the Congress would grant the Secretary of War authority to lease the nitrate plant on such terms as would insure the largest production of nitrates, the entire property could begin to function. Such a division, I am aware, has never seemed to appeal to the Congress. I should also gladly approve a bill granting authority to lease the entire property for the production of nitrates.

I wish to avoid building another dam at public expense. Future operators should provide for that themselves. But if they were to be required to repay the cost of such dam with the prevailing commercial rates for interest, this difficulty will be considerably lessened. Nor do I think this property should be made a vehicle for putting the United States Government indiscriminately into the private and retail field of power distribution and nitrate sales.

CONSERVATION

The practical application of economy to the resources of the country calls for conservation. This does not mean that every resource should not be developed to its full degree, but it means that none of them should be wasted. We have a conservation board working on our oil problem. This is of the utmost importance to the future well-being of our people in this age of oil-burning engines and the general application of gasoline to transportation. . . .

IMMIGRATION

The policy of restrictive immigration should be maintained. Authority should be granted the Secretary of Labor to give immediate preference to learned professions and experts essential to new industries. The reuniting of families should be expedited. Our immigration and naturalization laws might well be codified.

WAGE EARNER

. . . Since 1922 increasing production has increased wages in general 12.9 per cent, while in certain selected trades they have run as high as 34.9 per cent and 38 per cent. Even in the boot and shoe shops the increase is over 5 per cent and in woolen mills 8.4 per cent, although these industries have not prospered like others. As the rise in living costs in this period is negligible, these figures represent real wage increases. . . .

WOMEN AND CHILDREN

The Federal Government should continue its solicitous care for the 8,500,000 women wage earners and its efforts in behalf of public health, which is reducing infant mortality and improving the bodily and mental condition of our citizens.

CIVIL SERVICE

The most marked change made in the civil service of the Government in the past eight years relates to the increase in salaries. The Board of Actuaries on the retirement act shows by its report that July 1, 1921, the average salary of the 330,047 employees subject to the act was $1,307, while on June 30, 1927, the average salary of the corresponding 405,263 was $1,969. This was an increase in six years of nearly 53 per cent. On top of this was the generous increase made at the last session of the Congress generally applicable to Federal employees and another bill increasing the pay in certain branches of the Postal Service beyond the large increase which was made three years ago. This raised the average level from $1,969 to $2,092, making an increase in seven years of over 63 per cent. While it is well known that in the upper brackets the pay in the Federal service is much smaller than in private employment, in the lower brackets, ranging well up over $3,000, it is much higher. It is higher not only in actual money paid, but in privileges granted, a vacation of 30 actual working days, or 5 weeks each year, with additional time running in some departments as high as 30 days for sick leave and the generous provisions of the retirement act. No other body of public servants ever occupied such a fortunate position.

EDUCATION

Through the Bureau of Education of the Department of the Interior the Federal Government, acting in an informative and advisory capacity, has rendered valuable service. While this province belongs peculiarly to the States, yet the promotion of education and efficiency in educational methods is a general responsibility of the Federal Government. A survey of negro colleges and universities in the United States has just been completed by the Bureau of Education through funds provided by the institutions themselves and through private sources. The present status of negro higher education was determined and recommendations were made for its advancement. This was one of the numerous cooperative undertakings of the bureau. Following the invitation of Land Grant Colleges and Universities, the Bureau of Education now has under way the survey of agricultural colleges, authorized by Congress. The purpose of the survey is to ascertain the accomplishments, the status, and the future objectives of this type of educational training. It is now proposed to undertake a survey of secondary schools, which educators insist is timely and essential.

PUBLIC BUILDINGS

We have laid out a public building program for the District of Columbia and the country at large running into hundreds of millions of dollars. Three important structures and one annex are already under way and one addition has been completed in the City of Washington. In the country sites have been acquired, many buildings are in course of construction, and some are already completed. Plans for all this work are being prepared in order that it may be carried forward as rapidly as possible. This is the greatest building program ever assumed by this Nation. It contemplates structures of utility and of beauty. When it reaches completion the people will be well served and the Federal city will be supplied with the most beautiful and stately public buildings which adorn any capital in the world.

THE AMERICAN INDIAN

The administration of Indian affairs has been receiving intensive study for several years. The Department of the Interior has been able to provide better supervision of health, education, and industrial advancement of this native race through additional funds provided by the Congress. The present cooperative arrangement existing between the Bureau of Indian Affairs and the Public Health Service should be extended. The Government's responsibility to the American Indian has been acknowledged by annual increases in appropriations to fulfill its obligations to them and to hasten the time when Federal supervision of their affairs may be properly and safely terminated. The movement in Congress and in some of the State legislatures for extending responsibility in Indian affairs to States should be encouraged. A complete participation by the Indian in our economic life is the end to be desired. . . .

PORTO RICO

Due to the terrific storm that swept Porto Rico last September, the people of that island suffered large losses. The Red Cross and the War Department went to their rescue. The property loss is being retrieved. Sugar, tobacco, citrus fruit, and coffee, all suffered damage. . . .

DEPARTMENT OF JUSTICE

It is desirable that all the legal activities of the Government be consolidated under the supervision of the Attorney General. In 1870 it was felt necessary to create the Department of Justice for this purpose. During the intervening period, either through legislation creating law officers or departmental action, additional legal positions not under the supervision of the Attorney General have been provided until there are now over 900. Such a condition is as harmful to the interest of the Government now as it was in 1870, and should be corrected by appropriate legislation.

SPECIAL GOVERNMENT COUNSEL

In order to prosecute the oil cases, I suggested and the Congress enacted a law providing for the appointment of two special counsel. They have pursued their work with signal ability, recovering all the leased lands besides nearly $30,000,000 in money, and nearly $17,-000,000 in other property. They find themselves hampered by a statute, which the Attorney General construes as applying to them, prohibiting their appearing for private clients before any department. For this reason, one has been compelled to resign. No good result is secured by the application of this rule to these counsel, and as Mr. Roberts has consented to take reappointment if the rule is abrogated I recommend the passage of an amendment to the law creating their office exempting them from the general rule against taking other cases involving the Government. . . .

CONCLUSION

The country is in the midst of an era of prosperity more extensive and of peace more permanent than it has ever before experienced. But, having reached this position, we should not fail to comprehend that it can easily be lost. It needs more effort for its support than the less exalted places of the world. We shall not be permitted to take our ease, but shall continue to be required to spend our days in unremitting toil. The actions of the Government must command the confidence of the country. Without this, our prosperity would be lost. We must extend to other countries the largest measure of generosity, moderation, and patience. In addition to dealing justly, we can well afford to walk humbly.

The end of government is to keep open the opportunity for a more abundant life. Peace and prosperity are not finalities; they are only methods. It is too easy under their influence for a nation to become selfish and degenerate. This test has come to the United States. Our country has been provided with the resources with which it can enlarge its intellectual, moral, and spiritual life. The issue is in the hands of the people. Our faith in man and God is the justification for the belief in our continuing success.

BIBLIOGRAPHICAL AIDS

BIBLIOGRAPHICAL AIDS

The emphasis in this and subsequent volumes in the Presidential Chronologies series will be on the administrations of the presidents. The more important works on other aspects of their lives, either before or after their terms in office, are included since they may contribute to an understanding of the presidential careers.

The following bibliography is critically selected. The student might also wish to consult Reader's Guide to Periodical Literature and Social Sciences and Humanities Index (formerly International Index) for recent articles in scholarly journals.

Additional Chronological information not included in this volume because it did not relate directly to the president may be found in the Encyclopedia of American History, edited by Richard B. Morris, revised edition, (New York, 1965).

Asterisks after titles refer to books currently available in paper back editions.

SOURCE MATERIALS

The major collection of materials concerning Coolidge is housed in the Calvin Coolidge Memorial Room of Forbes Library, Northampton, Massachusetts. Included there are texts of practically all of his speeches and proclamations, presidential and otherwise; transcripts of his presidential press conferences and other informal statements, and his correspondence as governor and Vice President. Both Coolidge and his wife contributed family photos, souvenirs and other mementos to the collection.

Some 284 manuscript boxes and three volumes of correspondence are included in the Coolidge Presidential Papers in the Library of Congress. Microfilm copies of these papers are in the Forbes Library.

BIOGRAPHIES

Coolidge, Calvin. The Autobiography of Calvin Coolidge. New York, 1929. Generally regarded as bland, impersonal and unrevealing.

However, biographer William Allen White calls the autobiography "unbelievably clarifying" if read with a knowledge of the events behind certain paragraphs.

Fuess, Claude M. Calvin Coolidge, Man from Vermont. Boston, 1940. Competently and sympathetically written by Coolidge's official biographer who regarded him as a highly qualified judge of men, politician and executive.

McCoy, Donald R. Calvin Coolidge: The Quiet President. New York, 1967. Well-written and well-researched, this biography by professor of history McCoy is designed as a reassessment of Coolidge and his Administration.

White, William Allen. A Puritan in Babylon: The Story of Calvin Coolidge. New York, 1938. This excellent biography by the famed Republican sage of Emporia, Kansas, is a study of Coolidge "as a part of his times" and an attempt to capture the real personality of the wooden-faced President.

ESSAYS

The essay by Allan Nevins in the Dictionary of American Biography gives a broad view of the concerns of government during Coolidge's administration. Equally instructive, though not in such depth, is the article in Encyclopedia Americana by Donald R. McCoy, a biographer of Coolidge.

Bates, J. Leonard. "The Teapot Dome Scandal and the Election of 1924," in American Historical Review, LX, January 1955, 303 ff.

Bradford, Gamaliel. "The Genius of the Average," in The Quick and the Dead, Boston, 1931, 221 ff. Speculates on the "essential elements" of Coolidge's character.

Glad, Paul W. "Progressives and the Business Culture of the 1920s," in Journal of American History, LIII, June 1966, 75 ff.

Hoffman, Frederick J. "The Temper of the Twenties," in Minnesota Review, I, Fall 1960, 36 ff.

Lathem, Edwin Connery. Meet Calvin Coolidge: The Man Behind the Myth. Brattleboro, Vermont, 1960. Contains all or parts of 34 essays by knowledgeable contemporaries and associates.

Leighton, Isabel, ed. The Aspirin Age. New York, 1949. A collection of
10 essays on major aspects of the decade.

Link, Arthur S. "What Happened to the Progressive Movement in the
1920's," in American Historical Review, Vol. 64, July 1959,
849 ff.

Russell, Francis. "The Strike That Made a President," in American
Heritage, October 1963, 91 ff.

White, William Allen. "What Demos Wished on Us," in Masks in a
Pageant, New York, 1928, 435 ff.

FOREIGN POLICY UNDER COOLIDGE

Adler, Selig. The Isolationist Impulse: Its Twentieth-Century Reac-
tion. New York, 1957.* Designed for the general public as well as
the specialist.

Adler, Selig. The Uncertain Giant: 1921-1941: American Foreign Policy Between the Wars. New York, 1965.* For the general reader.

Bemis, S.F. The Latin American Policy of the United States. New
York, 1943.

Duroselle, Jean-Baptiste. From Wilson to Roosevelt; Foreign Policy
of the United States, 1913-1945. Cambridge, 1963. This translation
of the French political scientist's work includes sections on
Hughes and Kellogg.

Ellis, L. Ethan. Frank B. Kellogg and American Foreign Relations,
1925-1929. New Brunswick, 1961. Kellogg is characterized as a
"busy mediocrity."

Ellis, L. Ethan. Republican Foreign Policy, 1921-1933. New Brunswick, 1968.

Feis, Herbert. The Diplomacy of the Dollar: First Era, 1919-1932.
New York, 1966.*

Ferrell, Robert H. Frank B. Kellogg and Henry L. Stimson, 1925-
1933 (Vol. XI, The American Secretaries of State and Their Diplomacy). New York, 1963.

Ferrell, Robert H. Peace in Their Time: The Origins of the Kellogg-Briand Pact. New Haven, 1952.* The basic text on the subject.

Fleming, D.F. The United States and World Organization, 1920-1933. New York, 1938.

Hicks, John D. Republican Ascendency, 1921-1933. New York, 1960.* Contains much on foreign policy under Coolidge.

Johnson, Claudius O. Borah of Idaho. New York, 1936.* Borah was chairman of the Senate Foreign Relations Committee during the Harding-Coolidge era.

McDougall, Duncan M. World Power and New Problems, 1914-1930. New York, 1964.

McKenna, Marian C. Borah. Ann Arbor, 1961.

Moulton, Harold G., and Pasvolsky, Leo. War Debts and World Prosperity. Washington, 1932. The standard work.

Nevins, Allan. The United States in a Chaotic World, 1918-1933. New Haven, 1950.

Nicolson, Harold. Dwight Morrow. New York, 1935. Insights on United States-Mexico relationship.

Stimson, H.L. American Policy in Nicaragua. New York, 1927.

Tate, Merze. The United States and Armaments. Cambridge, 1948.

Timmons, Bascom N. Portrait of an American, Charles G. Dawes. New York, 1953.

Whitaker, Arthur P. The Western Hemisphere Idea; Its Rise and Decline. Ithaca, 1954.*

PEOPLE AND CURRENTS IN COOLIDGE'S ERA

Abels, Jules. In the Time of Silent Cal. New York, 1969. A retrospective history of the 1920s.

Allen, Frederick Lewis. Only Yesterday. New York, 1957.* (2nd ed.) A major work on the social history of the United States from 1918 to the 1929 crash.

Asbury, Herbert. The Great Illusion: An Informal History of Prohibition. Westport, Connecticut, 1950.

Bernstein, Irving. The Lean Years: A History of the American Worker,
1920-1933. Boston, 1960.*

Chalmers, David M. Hooded Americanism. New York, 1965.

Daniels, Jonathan. The Time Between the Wars. Garden City, 1966.
Authoritative close-up views of many on the Washington scene
in the 1920s.

Fite, Gilbert C. George Peek and the Fight for Farm Parity. Norman,
Oklahoma, 1954.

Furniss, Norman F. The Fundamentalist Controversy, 1918-1931.
New Haven, 1954.

Garraty, John A. Henry Cabot Lodge: A Biography. New York, 1953.
Based on Lodge's own papers.

Hoover, Irwin H. Forty-two Years in the White House. Boston, 1934.
Reminiscences of a head usher.

LaFollette, B.C. and F. Robert M. LaFollette. New York, 1953.

Leuchtenburg, William E. The Perils of Prosperity, 1914-32. Chicago,
1958.*

Lubell, Samuel. The Future of American Politics. New York, 1952.*

MacKay, Kenneth. The Progressive Movement of 1924. New York,
1947.

Martin, Joseph. My First Fifty Years in Politics. New York, 1960.
Among memories, the Speaker of the House recalls his friendship with Coolidge.

Merz, Charles. The Dry Decade. Garden City, 1931. A basic work on
prohibition.

Moos, Malcolm, ed. A Carnival of Buncombe. Baltimore, 1956. A
collection of H.L. Mencken's biting political pieces on Coolidge
and others.

Nevins, Allan, and Hill, Frank. Ford: Expansion and Challenge: 1915-
1932. New York, 1957. On the automobile industrialist.

Noggle, Burl. Teapot Dome: Oil and Politics in the 1920s. New York, 1962.* Goes into the roots of what became the major scandal of the 1920s.

O'Connor, Harvey. Mellon's Millions, The Biography of a Fortune; The Life and Times of Andrew W. Mellon. New York, 1933.

Prothro, James W. Dollar Decade: Business Ideas in the 1920s. Baton Rouge, 1954.

Quint, Howard H., and Ferrell, Robert H., eds. The Talkative President: The Off-the-Record Press Conferences of Calvin Coolidge. Amherst, 1964.

Randel, William P. The Ku Klux Klan; A Century of Infamy. Philadelphia, 1965.

Ross, Ishbel. Grace Coolidge and Her Era. New York, 1962.

Ross, Walter S. The Last Hero: Charles A. Lindbergh. New York, 1968.

Schlesinger, Arthur M., Jr. The Crisis of the Old Order 1919-1933. Boston, 1957.*

Schriftgiesser, Karl. This Was Normalcy. Boston, 1948.

Soule, George. Prosperity Decade: From War to Depression, 1917-1929. New York, 1947.*

Sullivan, Mark. Our Times, The United States, 1900-1925, VI, The Twenties. New York, 1935.

Werner, M.R., and Starr, John. Teapot Dome. New York, 1959.

NAME INDEX

TITLES IN THE OCEANA
PRESIDENTIAL CHRONOLOGY SERIES
Reference books containing
Chronology—Documents—Bibliographical Aids
for each President covered.
Series Editor: **Howard F. Bremer**

*   96 pages, \$3.00/B
** 128 pages, \$4.00/B
*** 160 pages, \$5.00/B